Advance praise for The Father's Love

"Rick Sodmont gives us a look behind the veil into the heavenlies, the supernatural realm, as he describes his incredible encounters with the living God. Rick is a man who has been literally touched by the love of God and speaks from his own experience—not just theory or intellect.

In this book, you will learn about the love language of heaven—intimacy with God. You will have a deeper understanding of the love God has for each one of us. As you grasp the truths presented here, you can learn to walk in love just as God intended."

—**Gary Oates**, Gary Oates Ministries and author of *Open My Eyes Lord*

"I just read Rick Sodmont's new book, *The Father's Love*. I read it in one setting, and was surprised at what God had done on one of our trips to Rick. The book was very helpful and enjoyable. I found good principles for living a more prophetic life.

I believe this book is very important to read to build your faith and hunger for more of God. There was great discernment as well as great drama in regard to Rick's experiences in the Holy Spirit. I believe it is the kind of book that reading it will make you hungry for a closer walk with God. I recommend you buy it and read it. You will not be the same."

—**Randy Clark**, Global Awakening Ministries and author of *Lighting Fires* and *There is More*

The Father's Love

The Father's Love

Richard A. Sodmont

iUniverse, Inc.
New York Bloomington Shanghai

The Father's Love

Copyright © 2008 by Richard A. Sodmont

All rights reserved. No part of this book may be used or reproduced by any means, graphic, electronic, or mechanical, including photocopying, recording, taping or by any information storage retrieval system without the written permission of the publisher except in the case of brief quotations embodied in critical articles and reviews.

iUniverse books may be ordered through booksellers or by contacting:

iUniverse
1663 Liberty Drive
Bloomington, IN 47403
www.iuniverse.com
1-800-Authors (1-800-288-4677)

Because of the dynamic nature of the Internet, any Web addresses or links contained in this book may have changed since publication and may no longer be valid.

The views expressed in this work are solely those of the author and do not necessarily reflect the views of the publisher, and the publisher hereby disclaims any responsibility for them.

All scripture quotations are from the New International Version of the Bible Copyright 1990 by Zondervan.

ISBN: 978-0-595-50144-1 (pbk)
ISBN: 978-0-595-49682-2 (cloth)
ISBN: 978-0-595-61390-8 (ebk)

Printed in the United States of America

To my Heavenly Father—for revealing his love to me in so many wonderful ways.

To Jesus Christ, my Lord and Savior—for giving his life that I might have life.

To the Holy Spirit—for directing my paths and inspiring me to write this book.

Contents

Acknowledgements xi
Introduction xiii
CHAPTER 1	The Adventure Begins 1
CHAPTER 2	How Much Do You Want? 6
CHAPTER 3	Then Suddenly 12
CHAPTER 4	Yet Another Surprise 16
CHAPTER 5	The Church View 25
CHAPTER 6	Earthly Fathers 33
CHAPTER 7	Love that Overcomes 38
CHAPTER 8	Secure in His Love 48
CHAPTER 9	The Father's Heart 53
CHAPTER 10	The Prodigal 66
CHAPTER 11	The Father's Will 73
CHAPTER 12	What About Me? 79
CHAPTER 13	Fatherhood 88
CHAPTER 14	Sonship 95

Acknowledgements

Tina, my wife—for loving me and supporting me through this journey of life.

Stephanie, Robin, Jessica, and Jacob, my children—for teaching me so much about the Father's love through their experiences.

Kevin Stock, my pastor—for instilling in me a hunger for more of God.

Randy Clark—for giving me the opportunity to experience the presence and power of God and for imparting into my life.

Gary and Kathi Oates—for recognizing the anointing on my life and encouraging me to step out and use it.

My Ministry Board—for taking care of so many of the details of ministry and giving me the time to be alone with God to receive revelation.

Ed Gibbons, my spiritual father—for imparting to me the wisdom that God has given him, some of which went into the writing of this book.

Dorey Marsh—for helping with the editing of this book.

Introduction

If God really loves me, then why does He allow so many negative things to occur in my life? Why doesn't He rescue me from such things? Maybe if I try harder I can be more pleasing to Him. Have I done enough to earn His favor?

These are the type of questions that I often used to ask, especially when my life was full of struggles and disappointments. When things were going good in my life, I felt it was because I had been pleasing to God and had earned His love. But when things went sour, I incorrectly discerned that I must have failed Him in some manner and disqualified myself from His love.

These are the same questions that countless others have asked me over my years of ministry. And these are the same incorrect conclusions that many people have come to, based mostly on their performance instead of what God accomplished for us in sending His Son to die on the cross for our sakes.

In today's society, we are judged by our performance in every area of life. Children are rewarded for their obedience and punished for their disobedience. Athletes are rewarded with starting positions and huge salaries for being better than the others on the team. Students are graded according to their performance. Even on our jobs, we are rewarded with promotions and higher salaries for performing well, and demoted to lower positions for failing.

But as it relates to the kingdom of heaven, **we are all loved the same.** This unconditional love is not based on our performance. It is simply based on God's love for us because we are His children.

Consider the Apostle Paul. He was a major recipient of God's love and grace, even though he had done absolutely nothing to earn it or deserve it. Actually, he did everything he could to oppose the name of Jesus. He had many Christians put in prison or even put to death. He said he was obsessed against them. This was his condition when Jesus appeared to him on his way to Damascus.

Can you imagine the shock that Paul must have felt when he asked, "Who are you Lord?" and Jesus replied, "I am Jesus, whom you are persecuting?" He must have been gripped with fear when he lost his sight. What horrific punishment awaited him in the hands of this angry God that he had been opposed to?

But instead of punishment, Paul received grace. Judging by his performance, Paul should have been thrown directly into the pit of hell. Instead, he was loved. What kind of God would grant love and favor to such a man as this, who in his religious zeal was actually an enemy of Jesus? It is the same God who loves us and desires to pour out his grace upon us, even though we don't deserve it either.

You see, God's love for us is not based on our performance, it is based solely on the fact that we are his creation and He desires for all of us to come into relationship with Him. And the ultimate expression of His love for us is found in the sending of His Son Jesus to die on the cross and pay the penalty for our sins, in order that we might be reconciled to Him.

1 John 3:16—This is how we know what love is: Jesus Christ laid down his life for us.

I have been working in deliverance and inner healing ministry for about twelve years now, and the issue of whether or not God loves us unconditionally is one of the biggest issues that I deal with in the lives of people. It is a foundational truth that must be established in the hearts of people if they are ever going to move on to bigger things in the Lord. There are so many people who struggle with rejection and who are not secure in the love of their heavenly Father. There are many others who live in fear and are constantly trying to avert God's judgment by performing better than others.

It is an issue that I first had to deal with in my life, and now God has released me to be able to help others. Through my personal struggles, through attending various seminars and conferences on these issues, through reading other books on this subject, and through ministering to people on an individual basis for many years now, I hope to impart the revelation that I have received concerning the Father's love to all who read this book.

As I have traveled across the United States and around the world, I am amazed at how many people, even Christians, have no concept of who God the Father really is and what He is really like. They have no idea how much He loves them and how compassionate and caring He is toward them. But the fact of the matter is that God loves all of us more than we can ever imagine.

Many people have the wrong image of God based upon what they have been taught about Him throughout their lives. Some of this has come from all the trials and struggles that people have gone through in their lives. Some have received this false image through the experiences they have had with their own earthly fathers. Some have been deceived by the teachings of the world and the world system, and many have been deceived by the erroneous teachings of the church.

This book is an attempt to reveal the true nature and character of our loving Father and to expose some of the false images of Him that have been presented to us. It is based on personal encounters that I have had with the Father and on revelation that He has given me over the years. It is also based on the truth of God's holy word, the scriptures.

I pray that the Spirit of wisdom and revelation will come upon you as you read this book, that you might come to know Him better. I invite each of you to seek the Lord for your own personal encounters as you read. The Bible declares that the testimony of Jesus is the spirit of prophecy. **Revelation 19:10.** Therefore, as you read my testimony, I believe God will release a prophetic anointing that can empower you to experience Him as I have.

I also believe God will impart to you a revelation of His love that is not based on your human effort, but on His divine will. God is not a respecter of persons. He loves everyone equally. And scripture says that in the last days, God will pour out His Spirit on all flesh. That includes you.

Acts 2:17-21—In the last days, God says, I will pour out my Spirit on all people. Your sons and daughters will prophesy, your young men will see visions, your old men will dream dreams. Even on my servants, both men and women, I will pour out my Spirit in those days, and they will prophesy. I will show wonders in the heaven above and signs on the earth below, blood and fire and billows of smoke. The sun will be turned to darkness and the moon to blood before the coming of the great and glorious day of the Lord. And everyone who calls on the name of the Lord will be saved.

I also want to encourage you to spend a few moments in prayer and ask the Father to remove all of the lies and false images that exist in your mind about Him before you read any further. I ask that you approach this book with an open heart and mind to receive all that God has for you. I truly believe that if you catch this revelation, it will revolutionize your Christian walk and experience.

You will be set free to become who the Father has called you to be and to fulfill all He has called you to do. You will never be able to love others the way that God wants you to unless you first love yourselves. And you will never truly love yourselves until you experience and embrace the Father's love for you.

1

The Adventure Begins

I had received the call of God into full time ministry in 1994, but by 2002, I was still working as a foreman for an electrical construction company. While employed there for close to fifteen years, God had used me on many occasions to minister to other people, bringing salvation, healing, and deliverance to men right on the job site.

During that time, I spent three and a half years in formal ministry training through my denomination. And as previously stated in the introduction, I had also received much training through seminars, conferences, books, and personal experiences.

I also spent much of my free time doing part-time ministry, mostly in my home state of Pennsylvania. So in one sense, I already considered myself to be in full time ministry. But I knew that God had other plans for me. I also knew that God was using this time to train me and equip me for bigger things.

Because of the nature of the construction industry, many times we were required to travel considerable distances away from home to work. In the spring of 2002, I found myself working on several jobs around Harrisburg, Pennsylvania. My brother Chris worked for the same company and the two of us were staying together through the week and then traveling back home on weekends.

Chris and his wife, Patty, had heard that Randy Clark was moving to Harrisburg and that he was going to be headquartered at a place called Life Center. And one day while we were at work, we met a man who lived near Life Center and he gave us directions on how to get there. So we decided to check it out.

The following week we were in the sanctuary of Life Center for the Wednesday night service. The service was a combination of worship and prayer, which was a little unusual for us. But in the middle of one of the songs, I heard the Lord say to me, "I want you to go to Brazil with Randy Clark." I replied, **"Who's Randy Clark?"**

Looking back I later realized that I had heard of Randy before but didn't really know anything about him. Part of the ministry training that I had received was from Bill and Barbara Cassada, who had traveled on many missions trips overseas with Randy. Though they had taught me much of Randy's teaching, I really didn't know Randy personally and didn't know much about him.

The Lord then said that he would introduce Randy to me when I arrived in Brazil. I asked several people about Randy, including Chris and Patty, who led me to his website and six months later I found myself in Brazil shaking hands with Randy Clark. Randy has an international ministry called Global Awakening and travels the world preaching the gospel, healing the sick, delivering the oppressed, and training others to do the same.

Leading up to the trip, I found myself both tremendously excited and a little bit afraid at the same time. I had never traveled outside of the United States before. This would be a whole new experience for me, and many questions began to run through my mind.

What would it be like? What would the people be like? Am I truly ready for this type of ministry experience? Though I had many questions, I sensed that this was the start of the really big things that God had planned for me. I also had enough faith in Him that if He called me to do this, He would protect me and give me everything I needed to accomplish His will on this trip.

The first couple of days in Brazil were really awesome. We would hold several services a day that would begin with worship, followed by preaching, and ending with the whole ministry team being released to do the work of the kingdom. Randy had laid hands on all of us and imparted his anointing to us. People were being saved, healed, and delivered like I had never seen in my entire life. **About 75 percent of the people that I was praying for were being healed, which totally amazed me.**

I was just a simple country boy, and though I had seen some miracles in America, it was nothing compared to what I was now experiencing. The revelation that God was giving to me was incredible. And the love that God was pouring into my heart for the Brazilian people was overwhelming. I found myself in tears on many occasions.

God also took me to a whole new level in intercession. God was speaking to me and giving me visions about the spiritual realm and the strongholds we were up against. He was showing us how to tear them down through the power of the Holy Spirit.

It was like living in the book of Acts. I prayed for a man who had a cancerous tumor on his neck about the size of a softball. He had been given only a few months to live. He was desperate. I watched the tumor disappear right in front of my eyes! Tears of joy ran down his face and mine. We gave glory to God!

Another man came to me whose right leg was about 3 inches longer than his left one. As a result, his back was all messed up. I asked God to allow his left leg to grow as long as the right one. Suddenly, as I kept praying for him, a heard a noise that sounded like a bone cracking. I watched in amazement as his leg began to grow. It grew until it was the same length as the other one. I also prayed for his back to be healed from the damage caused by years of walking on legs of different length. The man left that night completely healed. Praise God!

I prayed for a woman who had cancer in her ovaries. She was suffering with a lot of pain. As I prayed, she could feel electricity shooting up and down her legs and into her abdomen. I commanded the cancer to go in the name of Jesus. She left there with no pain and believed she was completely healed.

I prayed for a young girl who had epilepsy and was always having seizures. As soon as I laid hands on her and began to pray, she began manifesting an evil spirit. She was shaking violently and horrible shrieks were coming out of her mouth. I commanded the spirit of epilepsy to leave her in the name of Jesus. She instantly calmed down and her whole countenance changed. I continued to soak her in prayer and released the peace of God into her. She left feeling and looking great.

In my heart, I knew this was what I was called to do. I kept crying out for more of God in my life. I wanted more love, more power, and more of Jesus in my life. **I could no longer be satisfied with "church as usual."** I had to have more. I had more hunger and thirst in me for God than I had ever known before. I couldn't get enough. The scriptures were coming alive in me. They were no longer just words on a page. They were life to me! God was speaking to me more clearly than ever before. I realized that this is what the Christian life is supposed to be like!

2

How Much Do You Want?

It was Saturday evening and our team had gathered to pray for the sick at an outdoor meeting in Belem, Brazil. We had gathered in the tent, and just before the ministry time, I asked one of the team leaders, Richard Holcombe, to pray for me because I was hungry for more of God's love and power.

Richard was a man whom God had used to prophesy to Randy Clark some years earlier regarding Randy's significant role in the revival meetings that were about to start in a church in Toronto, Canada. Randy then went to Toronto and God used him to start a revival there that continues to this day.

I started to shake violently when Richard laid his hands on me and began to pray. He was speaking prophetically into my life. I was shaking so hard that the people around me couldn't hold me up anymore, so they laid me on the floor.

After about twenty minutes the shaking calmed down, but I was paralyzed and couldn't get off the floor. I couldn't move a muscle in my body. I asked God what he was doing to me but received no reply. Finally, I was able to move a little but couldn't stand up, so I crawled across the floor to a chair and pulled myself up on it. Then I began to travail more violently than I ever had before. And God began to speak to me.

He asked, **"How much of me do you really want?"** As I was pondering this question He asked me another one. **"How bad do you want this anointing?"**

My first thought was that I wanted all of Him and all of His anointing. He said he would give it to me if I really wanted it. He also warned me that it would cost me everything. He said it would cost me my life. I sensed that it wasn't that I would be killed, but I would be required to lay down my life in service to Him.

God asked me again how much of Him I wanted and if I was sure that I really wanted it. He told me to weigh this decision carefully, because if I decided to accept this offer, I would never be the same. He would turn my life upside down. Then He told me to fast and pray for the next twenty-four hours but not to pray for anyone else because I had been consecrated wholly unto Him. Then He was silent.

My confidence in wanting more was wavering. I wasn't really sure if I wanted more after He had said this to me. I needed some time to count the cost. My spirit man was all for it, but my flesh was scared and wanted nothing to do with it. Incidentally, after that twenty-four hour period was over, every person I prayed for on the remainder of that trip was healed.

I sat on the chair for the next two hours, violently travailing and convulsing, while the rest of the team prayed for people. My stomach muscles hurt so bad I could barely stand it. I must have done a million stomach crunches. I was sweating profusely, and it was even getting difficult to breathe.

Then some of the other team members came and told me it was time to go over to the parking lot for the main service. They asked if I wanted to stay at the ministry tent or go over to the area for the main service. I told them that for some reason, **I just knew I had to go over there for the service!**

So two of them picked me up and carried me over to the parking lot and up onto the stage. They sat me down on a chair on the back of the stage. I was amazed that they did this for me as it was probably close to 250 yards from the tent to the parking lot, and I wasn't a small person who was easy to carry. I praise God for their willingness to get me to where God wanted me to be. At this point in time, I was totally exhausted from all of the travailing.

Then Randy Clark got up to speak. As he did, God pushed my head down in between my knees so far that I could barely breathe. I thought I was going to die. I thought, **"Lord, you're killing me."** He said, **"Yes, I am!"** Obviously, God was not physically killing me. He was working deep within me to set me free from things that would hinder my ability to fulfill my calling. There is a price to be paid for receiving the anointing of God. Though He freely gives it to us, He desires us to lay down our lives for Him.

Mark 8:34-35—Then he called the crowd to him along with his disciples and said: "If anyone would come after me, he must deny himself and take up his cross and follow me. For whoever wants to

save his life will lose it, but whoever loses his life for me and for the gospel will save it."

What about you today? Are you willing to lay down your life in service to God? Do you want more of Him in your life, or are you satisfied with mediocrity? Do you want His love, power, and glory to flow through you so that you can impact the lives of those around you? I can't answer that question for you; I can only speak for myself.

But I can tell you this; my life has never been the same since I made this decision to follow Him with all of my heart. He has taken me places in Him that most people only dream about. I have visited the heavenly realms on many occasions. I have grown deeply and madly in love with Jesus. I have seen Him do incredible things through me. I continue to receive revelation directly from the throne room of Heaven. He sends me all over the world to preach the good news of the kingdom, to heal the sick, and to drive out demons. I wouldn't trade it for anything.

But it comes with a cost. It requires laying down our own desires to pursue His. It requires our time, our effort, our finances, and everything about us. **Luke 14:28-32** speaks of counting the cost before we jump into something that we're not prepared for.

And then in verse 33, Jesus says, **"In the same way, any of you who does not give up everything he has cannot be my disciple."** So how bad do you want it? How much of him do you really want? Are you willing to lay down your life so that Jesus can take it up again and use it for His purposes? Or are you satisfied with the way things are? God has so much more for us if we would be willing to completely surrender to Him.

The issue is our hearts. There are things in our hearts that we don't even realize are there and God wants to deal with those issues. The more our hearts become like His, the more of His glory he can entrust to us. God knows that if these issues are not properly dealt with, it will leave the door open for the enemy to use those things against us somewhere down the road.

Even if we completely surrender ourselves to Jesus, He does not promise us a life without any struggles. On the contrary, He said in this life we would have many trials. He said anyone who would follow after Him would be persecuted. But He also promised that He would always be with us and that He would get us through those difficult times. And He uses those times to refine us into who He wants us to be.

I have been through many trials myself over the years. There were many times when I felt like giving up. And many times I thought about going back to the way things were before. Life was so much easier back then. But I also had no love, no power, and no anointing on my life back then. I accomplished little for the kingdom.

Through it all, I have seen God's faithfulness. He has taken me through every valley and over every hurdle. And I wouldn't trade my life for anything now. I now live in a loving relationship with my Father in Heaven, with Jesus my beloved, and with the Holy Spirit. Nothing can compare to knowing God and living in relationship with Him every day!

So again I ask, what about you? How much of Him do you really want? Are you willing to pay the price to have more of Him in your life? I can assure you that though you will go through many difficult times, the blessedness of knowing Him and experiencing Him on a daily basis will far outweigh the light and momentary struggles you will face on this earth. So just go for it!

3

Then Suddenly ...

So there I was, sitting on a chair on the back of the stage in Belem, Brazil. I was oblivious to anything that was happening in the physical realm. **Then suddenly, it was if a veil had been removed from my eyes and I could see into the spiritual realm.**

There were demons everywhere, battling against the angels and tormenting the people. There were principalities gathered over the city. There were angels warring against the demons. There were angels ministering to the people. It was both an awesome and terrible sight to see. I had previously had some visions and seen a few things in the spiritual realm, but nothing like this. At that moment, the spiritual realm seemed clearer to me than the physical realm.

2 Corinthians 4:18—So we fix our eyes not on what is seen, but on what is unseen. For what is seen is temporary, but what is unseen is eternal.

Then I heard a trumpet blast from up in the heavens that sent a chill down my spine. I looked up and saw the heavens open over the parking lot where we were ministering. I saw a stairway begin to descend from Heaven. It was made of the purest gold, so pure it looked like glass. You could see through it. Then a red carpet rolled down the stairs. And angels began appearing on both sides of the stairs. The stairs came all the way down until they stopped just above the parking lot about seventy-five yards from where I was sitting. A platform of gold formed there.

Another trumpet blast turned my attention back to the top of the stairway. I saw the throne of Almighty God begin to descend down the stairway, with the Father seated on His throne. The throne just seemed to float down the steps. At this point in time in the physical realm, worship was going on in the service. I heard one of the angels cry out, **"God is enthroned on the praises of His people."**

I could hardly believe what I was seeing. The Lord, the Creator of Heaven and Earth, was descending to the platform that was only seventy-five yards away from me. As He descended, His glory became so powerful that it was all I could do to look at Him. His face was shining like the sun. He looked both ancient and young at the same time. I was awestruck!!

Then the stairs began to form again from the platform where God was seated all the way down to the front of the stage. The red carpet also came down, but it didn't stop at the front of the stage, it rolled all the way over to my feet. Again angels appeared on either side of the stairs and all the way across the stage to where I was seated.

I knew one of two things was about to happen. Either God was about to come down to me, or He was about to call me up to where He was. This thought blew me away and I began to weep violently. I began to cry out, **"Unclean, unclean, don't come any closer."** I felt much like the Prophet Isaiah did in when he also had a vision of the Lord.

Isaiah 6:5—"Woe to me!" I cried. "I am ruined! For I am a man of unclean lips, and I live among a people of unclean lips, and my eyes have seen the King, the Lord Almighty."

I looked back towards the Father to see what He was doing. I saw Jesus come right out of the Father and begin to descend the stairs toward me. I thought of the scripture where Jesus said, **"I and my Father are one."** I was still weeping and my nose was running but I couldn't even lift my arms to help myself. I kept crying out, "Unclean, unworthy, don't come any closer Lord." But He just kept coming. I couldn't stop Him.

He came over and stood directly in front of me. **The King of Kings and Lord of Lords was only two feet away from me!** Words cannot express how I felt at that moment, both terribly excited and terribly afraid. I wished I was dead, and I felt like I was. His glory was so powerful that I couldn't bear it any longer. Then an angel standing next to me handed me a piece of fruit and told me to eat it. He said it would help me withstand His glory.

So there I was, just a "little ole me" from Hastings, Pennsylvania, and the King of Glory is standing right in front of me. **How small and insignificant I felt in his presence!** Then Jesus reached inside of Himself and pulled out a crown. It was full of rubies, and diamonds, and all kinds of precious stones. He began to place the crown on my head. Once again I began to cry out that I was unclean and unworthy to receive it. But He kept moving it closer to my head.

I suddenly realized that this crown represented my calling and anointing in the Lord. I also realized that I hadn't even accepted the

Lord's offer yet, so I asked him to stop. He said that the decision had already been made. I said, "Lord, you told me to weigh this decision carefully, and I haven't decided if I wanted this yet." Again, He said that the decision had already been made. I didn't understand. I had not yet decided. So then He said, "I have searched your heart, and the decision has already been made." He knew my heart better than me.

Then He placed the crown on my head. This caused me to travail even harder than I already was. I told the Lord that I could not accept it because it belonged to him. He was the one who deserved to wear it. **I wanted to lay it at His feet and just worship Him!** But He told me that I must wear this crown the rest of my life. He told me to never take it off. It would be recognized by both Heaven and Hell. I was utterly in shock. I continued weeping and slobbering all over myself. This was almost too good to be true!

4

Yet Another Surprise

To my utter surprise, Jesus then turned sideways so as to be able to see me and the Father. Holding His left arm out toward me and His right one toward the Father, He began to speak. He said, **"Father, I present to you Richard Sodmont, one of our kings and priests."** I could not believe what I had just heard. It just couldn't be. It was too good to be true! But it was.

I mustered up enough strength and courage to look up at the Father. He was looking intently at me with a love I had never known before. Tears began to fill His eyes and run down His face. For the first time in a long time, I got the revelation of how deeply the Father loves us, how much He loves me! I wept and I wept as waves of His love just continued to wash over me. I have never experienced anything in my entire life as wonderful as His love.

Then it was if time had stopped. All of the angelic and demonic activity came to a halt. Everyone's eyes focused on the Father as they sensed He was about to speak. He pointed to me with his right hand and said, **"This is my beloved son, in whom I am well pleased."** I nearly died! This was too much to even try to comprehend.

How could He love a sinner like me so much? Doesn't He know what I'm really like? How could He possibly be pleased with me? This must be some sort of mistake! But all of the sudden many scriptures about His love for us were opened up to me, and I began to understand them correctly for the first time. Sorry, but I really have no words in my vocabulary to properly express the overwhelming love that I received from Him at that moment.

1 John 3:1—How great is the love that the Father has lavished on us that we should be called the children of God. And that is what we are.

The Father has given us His love without limit and without measure so that we could be reconciled to Him and be adopted into His family. The love that I was experiencing at that moment is the same love He has for all of us. He loves you just as much as He loves me or anyone else. Perhaps you have never experienced His love like I have, but that doesn't mean He doesn't love you.

The reason Jesus died on the cross **was not** to give us a fire escape from hell. It wasn't just so we could receive forgiveness from sin. It was so we could be restored back to our loving Father. It was to give us back what was lost in the garden when Adam and Eve fell into sin. It was to restore our relationship with God the Father, so that we could live in intimacy with Him.

His love doesn't call us to religion, it calls us to relationship! His greatest desire is to live in intimacy with us. And He sent His Son to be the ultimate expression of His love for us.

For those of you who continue to struggle with whether or not God loves you, it is imperative that you get this revelation. God loves you in spite of yourselves. He loves you in spite of your weaknesses and your sin. He loves you so much that He sent His Son to take the punishment for your sins. His love for you is not based on your performance, it is based on the performance of Jesus who fulfilled the law and gave Himself as a sacrifice for our sins.

The death and resurrection of Jesus is the ultimate proof of God's love for all of mankind. And we cannot do anything to earn His love. We don't deserve it. But He freely gives it to us and all He asks in return is that we receive it. He did all of that so that we could be reconciled to Him. He wanted a relationship with us so badly that He paid the penalty for our sins so we could now approach Him without fear or condemnation.

Romans 8:1—Therefore, there is now no condemnation for those who are in Christ Jesus.

On a separate occasion, when I was standing in front of the Father in the throne room of Heaven, He gave me this message to deliver to his people:

"Tell my people to wake up. Tell them to wake up. There are many in the church who are sleeping. They honor Me with their lips, but their hearts are far from Me. They worship Me in vain. They have a form of religion, but there are few who actually live in relationship with Me.

Tell them that what I desire the most is to have an intimate relationship with each one of them. I don't want their religious activities, I want a relationship. I want the kind of relationship that

exists between a husband and wife. I am your husband and you are My bride! Tell them that I love them all very much and I have no greater desire than to be intimate with each one of them. And then, out of that intimacy, I will empower them to be My witnesses.

I would love to come back and take each of my children home with Me right now, but the moment I do, I will be condemning millions of people to eternal damnation in hell. So tell my children to wake up."

Imagine that! Of all the messages that the Lord could have given me for His people in these days, He spoke about intimacy. He said he's tired of religion and religious practices. He said His people are sleeping. We are missing out on what God desires the most. He also said that if we would choose to be intimate with Him, He would empower us to be His witnesses. Many people in the church today want to see His power but aren't willing to seek Him to get it. He said all that most people have is religion, and there are few who actually have a relationship with him. That was a very sobering statement to me.

It reminds me of the words that Jesus spoke to the Pharisees and teachers of the law in **Mark 7:6-13:**

He replied, "Isaiah was right when he prophesied about you hypocrites; as it is written: 'These people honor me with their lips, but their hearts are far from me. They worship me in vain; their teachings are but rules taught by men.' You have let go of the commands of God and are holding on to the traditions of men."

And he said to them: "You have a fine way of setting aside the commands of God to observe your own traditions! For Moses said, 'Honor your father and your mother,' and 'Anyone who curses his father or mother must be put to death.' But you say that if a man says to his father or mother: 'Whatever help you might otherwise have received from me is Corban' (that is, a gift devoted to God), then you no longer let him do anything for his father or mother. Thus you nullify the word of God by your tradition that you have handed down. And you do many things like that."

I believe the heart of God is truly grieved today because of how religious the church has become. We have become more concerned with keeping our traditions than with loving God and loving others. Have you ever asked yourself why you do what you do? Are your religious practices mere traditions, or are they actually drawing you closer to God and others? Do you go to church, pray, worship God, read your Bible, and do other things because it's what you're supposed to do, or because you want to know him better? Sadly, I believe most people are missing out on a wonderful relationship with the Father, Son, and Holy Spirit because all they have is religious traditions.

Now, let's get back to the original encounter in Brazil. The demons shrieked with fear when the Father called me His son. They recognized the authority that I have as a child of God, and they trembled. The angels also acknowledged me as a co-laborer with them. My heart and mind were opened to see the world as God does. Paul stated in **2 Corinthians 5:16, "From now on we regard no one from a worldly point of view."** I began to see everything from a different perspective, from God's perspective. I was seeing the reality of the spiritual realm.

I began to see things as an heir to my Father's kingdom, instead of as a servant to my master. **I am the son of Almighty God, and he is my Father.** This changes everything! I began to serve the Lord out of love instead of duty or obligation. I didn't serve Him because I had to; I served Him because I wanted to. When I realized how much He loved me, how could I not obey Him! How could I not trust Him with my life!

There really are no words that I can tell you to describe the awesome love and peace that I was experiencing at that time. It was so overwhelming that I didn't even know how to respond to it. I began to ponder what I was experiencing. I was thinking to myself that I wish every person on the face of the earth could see this. If they only knew how much God loved them they would surely surrender their lives to Him.

I want to encourage all of you to begin to ask the Father right now for a revelation of His love for you. He loves all of us the same. He doesn't love me any more than He loves you. As the matter of fact, He loves all of us just as much as he loves Jesus, his Son. See **John 17: 23.** And until you get a revelation of His love, until you get this foundational truth established in your own heart, you will never be able to move on to the deeper things of God. And you will never fulfill His purposes for your life if you are constantly doubting His love for you.

Then I was allowed to see every thought coming from the mind of God. There were billions of thoughts leaving His head constantly. These thoughts flowed out to every person in that place, as well as all over the world. Do you realize that God is constantly speaking good thoughts over you? I watched a constant flow of thoughts go to every person in that place. They looked liked little gold capsules leaving His mind.

Some of His thoughts would get to their intended person, hit them in the head, and then fall to the ground. There were people there who didn't receive any of God's thoughts. There were people who received only a few of His thoughts. Even the people that I knew heard from God on a regular basis received only a small percentage of His thoughts. I was amazed by this.

Not only could I see His thoughts, but I could also understand them. I understood what He was speaking to the unbelievers in that place. I understood what He was speaking to the ministry team. I could pick out any thought flowing from God to another person and understand what He was saying to them. He was constantly telling them how much He loved them. He was speaking blessings over them. He was declaring His purposes for their lives to them. He was sending revelation about Himself to them. He was giving them wisdom and knowledge on how to deal with the situations in their lives. But sadly, most of His thoughts went unnoticed.

Sometime later, I asked the Lord to show me in the scriptures the reality of seeing a constant flow of His thoughts toward people. I did not want to be deceived in any manner. He told me to go to Psalms 139.

Psalms 139:17-18—How precious to me are your thoughts, O God! How vast is the sum of them! Were I to count them, they would outnumber the grains of sand. When I awake, I am still with you.

I also began to wonder exactly what type of ministry I would have and where I would be ministering. Then Jesus took me by the hand and said, "Come with Me." In an instant we were soaring up through the clouds. We went high enough into the atmosphere to see all of the continents, but were low enough to make out countries and states. We flew over North America and up to Pennsylvania, my home state. Jesus told me much of my ministry would be there. He also said He would send me to many other states to minister.

Then we flew over Africa and Jesus said He would also send me there. We flew over Southeast Asia, Russia, and the Ukraine. We flew over the Middle East and Great Britain. Jesus said I would minister in all of these places one day. He said my ministry would be known by my love for people and that many signs, wonders, and miracles would follow me wherever I went.

Then we flew back to Brazil and landed back on the stage. He said this would not be my last trip to Brazil. Since that trip, I have been back to Brazil five other times and have also ministered in Columbia, South America, and Ghana, Africa, as well as Florida, Maryland, Delaware, New York, Nevada, Arizona, and Washington, D.C.

Then Jesus went back into the Father. I was left slumping over in my chair, completely overwhelmed and exhausted. It was hard to comprehend what had just happened. One of the angels standing next to me handed me another piece of fruit and told me to eat it so that I would get my strength back. I then watched God save, heal, and deliver many people that night. This was one of the most incredible nights of my life!

I realize that I am sharing some incredible experiences with you in this book. It may be difficult for some to comprehend these things. But I want to assure you that none of these experiences go against the teaching of the scriptures.

5

The Church View

As previously stated in the introduction, there are many people who have the wrong concept of who God the Father really is and what He is really like. Throughout our lives we have been taught and/or experienced many things that have shaped our opinion of the Father. Unfortunately, much of this teaching and many of these experiences have given us a false image of Father God. These images are not based in truth, but are often based in lies from the enemy. And sometimes these lies have even come from the church.

For instance, many of the false perceptions of God that have come through the church often occur when our beliefs about God the Father today are based upon Old Testament theology. This can happen any time we incorrectly form an opinion about the Father based on the old covenant instead of the new one. Sometimes the church preaches works for salvation or for sanctification based on living up to the law instead of trusting in the grace of God. Even those who preach grace often mix it with works when it comes to certain areas of our lives, causing much confusion among the brethren. But consider the words of Jesus:

Luke 16:16—"The Law and the Prophets were proclaimed until John. Since that time, the good news of the kingdom of God is being preached, and everyone is forcing his way into it."

The old covenant ended with the coming of John the Baptist. Since that time, the good news of the kingdom is being preached. And remember, **the message of the kingdom is good news!** It's not a bunch of dos and don'ts, it's all about relationship. John's message was that the kingdom of heaven was near. Jesus also preached the message of the kingdom everywhere He went. But the days of the law and the prophets were over. The old covenant was given to make us conscious of sin and to show us our need for a Savior because no one could live up to the demands of the law.

Galatians 3:24-25—So the law was put in charge to lead us to Christ that we might be justified by faith. Now that faith has come, we are no longer under the supervision of the law.

God instituted a new and living covenant through which He now deals with men. It is a covenant based on grace, not law. It is a covenant entered into by faith, not observance of rules and regulations. It is a covenant whereby the grace of God and the Holy Spirit teach us to say no to ungodliness and worldly passions. It is not by human effort, or by living up to the law.

Romans 3:20-25—Therefore no one will be declared righteous in his sight by observing the law; rather, through the law we become conscious of sin. But now a righteousness from God, apart from law, has been made known, to which the Law and the Prophets testify. This righteousness from God comes through faith in Jesus Christ to all who believe. There is no difference, for all have sinned and fall short of the glory of God, and are justified freely by his grace through the redemption that came by Christ Jesus. God presented him as a sacrifice of atonement through faith in his blood.

The Apostle Paul also addressed this very issue in his letter to the Galatians.

Galatians 3:1-3—You foolish Galatians! Who has bewitched you? Before your very eyes Jesus Christ was clearly portrayed as crucified. I would like to learn just one thing from you: Did you receive the Spirit by observing the law, or by believing what you heard? Are you so foolish? After beginning with the Spirit, are you now trying to attain your goal by human effort?

I believe there is a natural tendency in man to always drift back to the law. We don't want to have to depend on someone else for our righteousness. We would rather do it ourselves. It is a self-righteous attitude that always leads us away from the grace of God and back into works.

A few years ago the Lord said to me, **"Those who choose to live under the law will suffer the consequences of the law."** Satan is a master in the law. And he demands that the consequences of the law be satisfied. When we choose the law instead of grace, we give him the legal right to hold us accountable to the law.

How often have you heard it preached that if you obey the Lord you will be blessed, and if you disobey Him you will be cursed? Deuteronomy 28 is a favorite passage of those who preach that message. But doesn't that go back to living under the law again? It is my personal belief that I am blessed because I am under grace, whether or not I am always obedient.

I am not saying that you should continue to sin or continue to live in sin because it doesn't matter, since we are under grace. See **Romans 6.** There are consequences to our sin. We often hurt ourselves and others by our disobedience. We can open the door for the enemy to harass us through our sin. That is one of the reasons that God gave us the Holy Spirit, to convict us of our sin and lead us back into obedience.

One of the problems with trying to live by the law is that it sometimes distorts our view of God the Father. We believe that every time we sin or fail Him, He is going to punish us. We view the Father as angry, distant, and unapproachable. But consider how the Lord described Himself even under the Old Covenant.

Exodus 34:6-7—And he passed in front of Moses, proclaiming, "The Lord, the Lord, the compassionate and gracious God, slow to anger, abounding in love and faithfulness, maintaining love to thousands, and forgiving wickedness, rebellion, and sin. Yet he does not leave the guilty unpunished."

Even under the Old Covenant, God presented Himself as very loving and compassionate. But many people that I have ministered to do not see Him that way. They see Him as a God of wrath who is just waiting to punish them. They quickly forget that Jesus took all of our punishment on the cross.

Isaiah 53: 4-6—Surely he took up our infirmities and carried our sorrows, yet we considered him stricken by God, smitten by him, and afflicted. But he was pierced for our transgressions, he was crushed for our iniquities; the punishment that brought us peace was upon him, and by his wounds we are healed. We all like sheep

have gone astray, each of us has turned to his own way; and the Lord has laid on him the iniquity of us all.

On another occasion the Lord said to me, **"If I ever punish you for your sins, then Jesus died for nothing."** Unfortunately, I deal with people all the time who believe that God is punishing them for their sins. Punishment has to do with wrath. But **Romans 5:9** tells us that we have been saved from God's wrath through the blood of Jesus. God does discipline us at times, but discipline is based in love, not wrath.

I was recently informed of a vision of the prophet Bob Jones where he saw some terrorist attacks coming upon America. A few weeks later while I was in worship one day, I was caught up in the spiritual realm and saw the details of one of these attacks. I saw all of the chaos and destruction caused by the attack. Many lives were destroyed. Then God spoke to me in the vision and said:

"Rick, this is not my judgment coming upon America. All judgment has been reserved until after Jesus returns. What you see before you is the work of the devil. And all of the natural disasters and destruction that you see occurring all over the world are also the work of the devil. You are living under the new covenant, under grace, not under the law any longer.

But many people will continue to blame me for what is happening. Even many pastors and prophets will stand behind their pulpits and declare that this is my judgment coming upon the earth because of the wickedness of men. But they are wrong. They are hearing from the second heaven. I take no delight in the death of the wicked and I do not wish that any should perish. I came to give

life not destroy it. These men will continue to give people the wrong image of who I am.

Because this is the work of the devil, it can be stopped, just like when Jesus would rebuke the storms and they would cease. If my people will cry out to me in intercession, and use the authority that I have given them in the heavenly realms, these disasters do not have to happen. So tell my people to cry out on behalf of this nation, and I will thwart the plans of the enemy."

Many people blame God for all of the bad things that happen in the world when usually these things are our own fault or the result of sin in general upon the earth. Some people mistakenly believe that some of these catastrophes are God's judgment coming upon America. But consider the words of Jesus:

John 12:47-48—"As for the person who hears my words but does not keep them, I do not judge him. For I did not come to judge the world, but to save it. There is a judge for the one who rejects me and does not accept my words; that very word which I spoke will condemn him at the last day."

My personal belief based on what the Lord spoke directly to me in the vision and based upon this scripture is that all judgment is being reserved until the last day. And it is reserved for those who ultimately reject Christ, not for those who accept him but don't live up to the law.

God has left us, **the church**, in charge of ruling the earth. Yet we stand around doing nothing while the enemy wreaks havoc all over the earth. We have allowed the enemy to kick God out of our government, and now we complain about the corruption in our government. We allowed him to kick God and His word out of our schools, and now we wonder why our kids are shooting each other. It's time that we, the church, take responsibility for the condition of the world.

2 Chronicles 7:14—"If my people, who are called by my name, will humble themselves and pray and seek my face and turn from their wicked ways, then I will hear from heaven and will forgive their sin and will heal their land."

It's time for the church to begin to cry out and intercede on behalf of the land. We are so quick to blame unbelievers for their sin when we are no better ourselves. We are constantly judging them and then we wonder why they won't join our ranks. We need to love them instead of judging them. It's time we humble ourselves and confess our own sin to God. It's time that we start showing the world what a loving Father we have instead of turning them away from God by our own false conceptions of who He is. We need to **re—present** Him to the world.

I have learned much about the Father through my own children. For instance, consider how often we blame God when things aren't going right in our lives? When my children would fall down and scrape their knee or elbow, they didn't come and ask me why I did that to them. They came and asked me to help them. And I would pray for them, put a band-aid on them, and do everything in my power to help them. I would pick them up on my lap and hold them until they stopped crying.

When one of their toys would break, they didn't ask how I could allow that to happen to them. They didn't ask, "Dad, don't you realize how important that toy was to me?" No, they came and asked me if I could fix it. And again, I would do anything I could to fix their toy, because I loved them and wanted to please them. What was important to them was important to me.

Why then do we, as God's children, blame Him when things go wrong or when we get hurt, instead of just going to Him and asking Him to help us? We should run to Him and cry out for help instead of blaming Him. He loves us, and as a Father, He will do everything in His power to help us. And He is not limited in His ability to help us like we are with our children.

You see, if you live on this earth then negative things are going to happen to you from time to time. But that doesn't mean they came from God or that God doesn't love you, just because you experienced something negative. It can be the result of living in a fallen world and sometimes, accidents just happen. But that doesn't mean that God doesn't love you.

It is critical that we know God as our loving Father, not as some angry God who is waiting to destroy us every time we mess up. And it is not enough to just know about His love, **we also must experience it.** My life changed forever through these encounters with Him because I truly experienced His love.

Sadly, there are many who have neither known nor experienced the Father's love. But I believe we are living in a day when God wants to reveal His love to us like never before. I encourage you to cry out to Him and ask him for a revelation of His love. It will change you too! Don't be satisfied until you are secure in His love.

6

Earthly Fathers

For many people, seeing God as a loving Father is beyond their capabilities. Some of that is due to incorrect teaching, but for many there are other underlying reasons why they cannot comprehend the love of the Father. **In many cases, it is directly related to the relationship that people have had with their earthly fathers.** Good, bad, or otherwise, our concept of God the Father has often been formed by the type of earthly father that we grew up with as children.

Unfortunately, a growing number of people that I minister to share with me the abuse that they have suffered at the hands of their earthly fathers. Many have suffered sexual abuse, physical abuse, verbal abuse, and/or mental abuse. Some have had fathers who were very harsh taskmasters. And as long as they obeyed the letter of his laws, everything was fine. But if they stepped out of line, there would be big trouble.

As a direct result of such abuse, people with this type of upbringing are oftentimes fearful of drawing close to their heavenly Father. They are afraid that He will treat them like their earthly dads did. They also view Him as a taskmaster who is waiting to punish them the moment they get out of line.

I have ministered to people whose earthly fathers would tell them how much they loved them but then proceed to abuse them in some manner. So when they are told of God the Father's love for them, they associate His love with abuse also and literally want nothing to do with it. **Many of them blame God for their circumstances.** They wonder how God could allow the abuse to happen if He loved them so much. But the truth is that it wasn't God's desire or plan to put them through such things; again, it is the work of the devil. He is the one who comes to steal, kill, and destroy.

Others have had earthly fathers who were addicted to alcohol, drugs, pornography, or even work. They saw how the whole family suffered from these addictions. Many times their dads weren't there for them when they needed them most. There are a lot of people who grew up with absentee fathers. And now they fear that their heavenly Father won't be there when they need Him. But nothing could be further from the truth. **God has promised that he would never leave us or forsake us.**

Many of these fathers became very violent while under the influence of alcohol or drugs. This type of violence often leads to separation or divorce, which rips families apart and can cause all sorts of problems in the children. Unfortunately, there are many people living in fatherless homes in a fatherless nation. They are living like orphans. **But Jesus said He would not leave us as orphans, but that He would come to us.** It is His heart's desire to comfort those who haven't known the real love of a father.

I also know many people whose fathers never abused them at all. But they never really showed them any love either. Though they knew their dads loved them, they never experienced their love and as a result they grew up not knowing how to receive love or give it away. They also struggle with receiving Father God's love and giving it away.

God is love and we were created in His image. We were created to be creatures of love. So it's in our very nature to want to receive love and also give it away. Those who have never experienced love think its ok to be the way they are, but they don't realize the blessings they are missing. I strongly believe that if such people ever truly experienced the Father's love, then they would see what they have been missing, and never want to go back to the way they are. That is why it's so important that we try to bring all people into encounters with the living God, not into religion.

The Bible is loaded with stories of people who had encounters with God. From Genesis to Revelation, you will find one interaction after another between God and men. Consider the relationship that Adam and Eve had with God in the Garden of Eden. God used to walk with them and talk with them in the cool of the day. They lived in perfect intimacy with Him. But when they sinned, that intimacy was broken. Their sin separated them from God, and they actually hid from Him. And so it is with all who have ever lived on the face of the earth, because all have sinned and fallen short of the glory of God.

But, before the creation of the world, God already had a plan to reconcile man to Himself. You see, God's purpose is not to just save us from the pit of hell. He loves us so much and so desires to live in an intimate relationship with us that He sent his Son to die in our place, so that the fellowship that was lost through sin could be restored. And He wants us to know Him as a loving Father, not an angry God who is waiting to destroy us or a harsh taskmaster who demands perfection. Consider the words of Paul to the Galatians:

Galatians 4:4-7—"But when the time had fully come, God sent his Son, born of a woman, born under law, to redeem those under law, that we might receive the full rights of sons. Because you are sons, God sent the Spirit of his Son into our hearts, the Spirit who calls out, 'Abba, Father.' So you are no longer a slave, but a son; and since you are a son, God has made you also an heir."

The type of relationship that God wants us to have with Him is like that which exists between a father and his children. Just as Jesus often referred to God as his Father, so God also wants us to see Him as a loving Father. I have known many people who view Jesus as very loving and compassionate, and have no problem being intimate with Him. But when it comes to the Father, they struggle. And their struggle usually goes back to the way their earthly father treated them. But consider what Jesus himself had to say about that.

John 10:30—"I and the Father are one."

John 14:9—"Anyone who has seen me has seen the Father."

Unfortunately, there are many people who believe that God the Father will only love them if they live up to a particular set of rules or regulations. **So they fall into the trap of wanting to do the work of the kingdom more than wanting to love the King of the kingdom.** They are motivated more by fear than they are by love. They fear being rejected by God and they fear failing him. What if they fail or don't do it good enough for him? This fear drives them into service instead of intimacy. Their concept of the Father is totally distorted and they become slaves to the law instead of sons of the King.

But what did Jesus say was the greatest commandment? **Matthew 22:36-40.**

"Teacher, which is the greatest commandment in the Law?" Jesus replied: "'Love the Lord your God with all your heart and with all your soul and with all your mind.' This is the first and greatest commandment. And the second is like it: 'Love your neighbor as yourself.' All the Law and Prophets hang on these two commandments."

What God desires the most is for all of us to live in a loving relationship with Him and with others. This can only happen when we know Him as our loving Father. For those who don't see Him as such, there needs to be a renewing of their minds. They need to be taught who God really is. And they need to experience His love. It is up to us, those who have experienced His love, to provide an atmosphere where they also can know and experience His love. We must do all we can to teach them correctly about their heavenly Father.

Though God desires our service and obedience, He would rather have our love. He doesn't want us to be motivated by fear, but by love. He knows that if He has our love, He will also have our obedience. His love is more powerful than our fear. Fear will only motivate us as long as the fear lasts, or until we are made even more fearful. But His love will motivate us for a lifetime. For you see, God's love is the most powerful force in the universe. It never fails!

7

Love that Overcomes

Romans 8:15—For you did not receive a spirit that makes you a slave again to fear, but you received the Spirit of sonship. And by him we cry, "Abba, Father."

I have often been asked questions like, "Why do you focus on the Father's love so much?" or "What's so important about experiencing the Father's love?" Well, simply put, it is His love that gives us the ability to overcome the world and all of the fear that we face in the world. There are so many people today who are absolutely paralyzed by fear. When we are fearful, we actually become slaves to that fear. Fear masters us and we act and react according to the fear that is over us. Only when we know and experience the Father's perfect love will we be able to overcome those fears.

1 John 4:18-19—There is no fear in love. But perfect love drives out fear, because fear has to do with punishment. The one who fears is not made perfect in love. We love because he first loved us.

We face many types of fear in this world: phobias, insecurity, fear of intimacy, fear of man, fear of rejection, traumas, fear of the unknown, fear of death, etc. These fears can paralyze us and keep us from fulfilling God's purposes in our lives. **But I have found that when I am secure in his perfect love, I am able to overcome any and all fear.** When we are secure in the Father's love, we will trust Him completely with our lives and do anything He asks us to do.

One of the biggest fears that I see in the church today is the fear of intimacy. This doesn't seem like it would be a very big issue for most people, yet in reality it is. Its roots go all the way back to the Garden of Eden. Consider how Adam and Eve lived before they fell into sin. They lived in perfect fellowship with God. But immediately upon sinning, they became filled with fear and actually hid from Him. They were now ashamed of their nakedness, and tried to cover themselves with fig leaves. Similarly, the fear of someone else finding out what we are really like keeps many of us in bondage.

John 3:20—"Everyone who does evil hates the light, and will not come into the light for fear that his deeds will be exposed."

Every religion on the face of the earth, except true Christianity, is "fig leaves." It is man's attempt to cover his nakedness. We are ashamed of the things we have done and don't want anyone else to find out about it. We are afraid to expose ourselves in front of God and in front of other people. We fear being found out. So we hide from God and from each other. We fear that God will punish us for our disobedience and we fear that others will reject us if they find out what we are really like. As long as we live under that fear, we will never seek help to overcome it. But consider what the Bible has to say about this.

James 5:16—Therefore confess your sins to each other and pray for each other so that you may be healed.

The path to healing, both physical and spiritual, is through confessing our sins to each other and praying for each other. That's what true intimacy is all about, not being afraid to expose ourselves to each other. And it's not just confessing sin to each other, but it also involves confessing our hurts and wounds to each other so that we can receive emotional healing. I encourage all of you to find someone that you can trust and begin sharing your hearts with each other and praying for each other so that you can be healed.

Unfortunately, the fear of exposing ourselves to other people is sometimes justified in the sense that too often we have been judged and condemned by those in the church. These are the very people who are supposed to be helping us, but many times they hurt us instead. It is critical that the church today provide an environment of love and acceptance so that those who are struggling can find help in their time of need.

If we can get to place where we are secure in His perfect love, then we will no longer fear being punished. As previously stated, Jesus already took all of the punishment that we deserve when He went to the cross. The cross alone was the final resting place of our punishment. **It is finished!** Jesus paid the full penalty for our sins.

We no longer need to fear being punished by our heavenly Father. On the contrary, it is His desire to help us overcome our sin and weaknesses. Only when we know His love will we be able to go to Him in times of failure to receive forgiveness and cleansing from our sin. Only then will we be able to boldly approach His throne of grace to find grace and mercy to help us in our time of need.

Another prevalent fear that I see in the church today is the fear of man. We literally fear what men may do to us. In many countries around the world, Christians do not have the religious freedom that we enjoy in this country. Many are being persecuted and even put to death because of their faith. Thankfully, it has not yet come to that in this nation. Even so, we are still fearful of being persecuted at the hands of men for our faith. Even those who seem to be very strong in the faith can succumb to this fear.

Consider the account of Elijah the prophet in 1 Kings, chapters 18 and 19. He had just pulled off the greatest victory of his life when he defeated the prophets of Baal on Mount Carmel. Can you imagine how he must have felt at the time? He showed great faith in God in challenging the enemy. And his faith probably grew tremendously when God showed up and consumed the sacrifice. He was literally on top of the mountain. Life couldn't be any better!

But then Jezebel threatened his life, and suddenly this great man of faith trembled with fear. Elijah was so afraid that he ran for his life. What happened to his great faith in God that he had a few moments before? It was swept away by the fear of what someone else might do to him. He was so gripped with fear that he actually wished that God would take his life. And there are many in the church today who have that same fear. This type of fear can literally paralyze us. It can keep us from fulfilling our destiny in the kingdom. Jesus himself said that we should not fear the ones who can kill our bodies, but fear him who has the power to throw us into hell.

It is imperative for people who deal with this type of fear to truly experience the Father's love. Only when they are secure in His love will they be able to move out in faith. Only when they trust the Father with their lives will they be completely obedient to Him, no matter what the cost. My children would do anything that I told them to when they were little, because they knew I loved them and they trusted me. This is the way God wants us to be with him; to trust him as a little child does.

Another fear that I want to address is the fear of rejection. Any time there is a love deficit in our lives it can lead to our feeling rejected. I haven't met anyone who hasn't dealt with rejection to some degree. Many people have been hurt so badly and carry such deep wounds in their hearts that they are terrified of being hurt again. As a result, they are afraid to trust anyone, including God, and they are afraid to allow anyone to get close to them again. They put up walls around their hearts to keep people from getting too close to them.

They are also afraid to witness to other people for fear of being rejected again. They have so much fear of what others will think of them, that they are unable to speak up and tell others about Jesus and what he has done for them. They are so fearful of being rejected by others that they become people pleasers instead of God pleasers.

Let me share with you some of the ways that rejection manifests in our lives, and also some of the ways that fear manifests in our lives. Those who deal with rejection and/or fear will typically have some or all of these symptoms. The following lists were compiled both from what I personally experienced in dealing with rejection and fear in my own life and from dealing with people in inner healing over the past twelve years.

Rejection

1. They are easily hurt and offended and tend to either lash out against those who reject them or give them the silent treatment.

2. They are always trying to please others at their own expense.

3. They are perfectionists.

4. They are often critical toward others.

5. They carry a lot of guilt and shame.

6. They often have suicidal thoughts.

7. They reject constructive criticism.

8. They are often in denial that they have this problem.

9. They like to draw attention to themselves.

10. They are very insecure.

11. They are afraid to trust anyone, including God.

12. They are often jealous of others who succeed.

13. They seek love in all the wrong places.

14. They often withdraw from fellowship with other believers.

15. They often harbor bitterness and unforgiveness towards those who have rejected them.

16. They often have addictions to drugs, alcohol, pornography, food, etc.

17. They often deal with depression.

18. They live in fear of being hurt and rejected again.

19. They have a hard time receiving or giving love.

20. They often have eating disorders like overeating, bulimia, or anorexia.

21. They are often rebellious.

Fear

1. They are often control freaks.

2. They often have nightmares.

3. They tend to worry about everything.

4. They are full of anxiety.

5. They are often paralyzed from doing things that are fearful to them.

6. They often use deception to cover their fear.

7. They fear intimacy. They don't want people to know they are fearful.

8. They often use anger and rage to try to control situations.

9. They have a difficult time trusting God for anything.

10. They think everyone is out to get them.

11. They may hear voices in their heads.

12. They often hear noises that cause them to be afraid.

13. They are afraid of things that they have no cause to be afraid of.

14. They often have trouble sleeping at night.

Again, the answer for overcoming fear and rejection is to be secure in God's perfect love. He has promised to **"never leave us or forsake us."** He has promised to provide for all of our needs. He has promised his protection. But just knowing these facts in our heads is not enough! We need to experience His perfect love in our hearts. And that will only happen through living in intimacy with Him and through experiencing His love as we walk through the trials and tribulations of our lives.

When men reject us, we need to learn to run to our heavenly Father for acceptance. He will always love us and accept us just the way we are. He alone will never reject us. When we are fearful, we need to run into His arms and allow Him to protect us and provide for us.

I too struggled with rejection throughout much of my life, even as an adult. And every time somebody would reject me in some manner, I would get wiped out. I would enter into a stage of depression and self pity. Many times I wished I was dead, just like Elijah did.

But through experiencing God's love, everything has changed for me. Now every time I feel rejected by someone, I run to God to find security in His perfect love. His love for me never fails, even when I fail Him. His love has completely liberated me and removed all fear! Nothing compares to knowing Him and living secure in His perfect love!

What about you? If you are still experiencing rejection or fear then I encourage you to go to the Father and ask Him to show you his perfect love. You can do this by reading scriptures that deal with rejection and fear, or by asking Him to speak to you personally about these things. Remember, the enemy wants you to believe his lies and live in fear and rejection. It is imperative that you learn to live according to the truth of God if you want to overcome these issues in your life.

Too often I've seen people who have been hurt by someone turn around and either try to hurt them back or take out their pain on a third party. The need for retaliation drives them into saying or doing things to hurt others in an attempt to cover their own pain. Bitterness and unforgiveness often go hand and hand with those who suffer with rejection.

But when we are filled with God's perfect love, we no longer feel the need to retaliate and we can no longer harbor feelings of bitterness and unforgiveness towards others. We realize the reason they said or did what they did was probably because of a lack of the Father's love in their own lives. **Love covers a multitude of sins.**

The following verses describe how our Father in heaven loves us and how He wants us to love others. Only when we know Him intimately and experience His perfect love for us, are we are able to love others the same way.

1 Corinthians 13:4-8—Love is patient, love is kind. It does not envy, it does not boast, it is not proud. It is not rude, it is not self-seeking, it is not easily angered, it keeps no record of wrongs. Love does not delight in evil but rejoices with the truth. It always protects, always trusts, always hopes, always perseveres. Love never fails.

The scriptures tell us that **God is love.** So I am going to ask you to read the previous verses again but this time as you read them, substitute the word "God" for the words "love" and "it". Do it over and over again until you get a revelation of God's love for you.

When you are finished with that, I want you to think about your love for others. How does it compare to these verses? Substitute your name for the words "love" and "it" and read it again. Does that really describe you, or would you be willing to admit that you're not there yet? If you can't honestly say that you love God and others that way, then ask the Father to change your heart so that you can love Him and others the same way He loves us.

8

Secure in His Love

One day while I was spending time with the Father, He led me to the account of the transfiguration of Christ in Matthew 17. I have heard many sermons on this passage and have preached on it many times myself. I sensed that God had a new revelation for me on this occasion. After reading it through a number of times without any deeper understanding, I asked God to reveal to me what it was He was trying to show me.

He spoke to me and said, "There's someone else besides the disciples who needed to hear that I loved Jesus and that I was pleased with him." As I thought about His statement, the only person who came to my mind was Jesus. So I asked the Father why it was so important for Jesus to hear and know that the Father loved him. He said it was because of what Jesus was about to go through at that time. He told me to go back to previous chapter and see what Jesus was about to do. So I did.

Matthew 16:21—From that time on Jesus began to explain to his disciples that he must go to Jerusalem and suffer many things at the hands of the elders, chief priests, and teachers of the law, and that he must be killed and on the third day be raised to life.

Can you imagine the anguish that Jesus must have felt as the time drew near for Him to be punished and die? That anguish was so great that Jesus was actually sweating drops of blood in the Garden of Gethsemane. The worst part of that might have been carrying the weight of the sins of the whole world. We must remember that He set aside all of His deity and became a man just like us. He was in all points tempted like we are, yet was without sin. Jesus needed to experience the Father's love because of what the Father was asking Him to do. He could not have done these things if He wasn't secure in His Father's love.

There are times in our lives when the Father will ask us to do things that will go far beyond our ability or desire to do. He may even ask us to lay down our lives for the sake of someone else. If we are not secure in His love to the point where we trust Him with even our very lives, then we will be too fearful to carry out His plans and fulfill His purposes in us. Fear will overtake us and keep us from our destinies. But His perfect love will drive out all fear and keep us moving forward with His plans.

As I was pondering these things in my heart, I remembered another occasion when the Father audibly spoke of His love for Jesus. It was immediately after Jesus was baptized by John in the Jordan River. Jesus was about to be led by the Spirit into the wilderness to be tempted by the devil. Then after that, He would begin his public ministry.

There is a definite need to be secure in the Father's love when we are going through wilderness experiences. It's during those times when it seems as though God is a million miles away from us, though He is actually very near. God often allows these experiences in our lives to prepare us for ministry to come, or to equip us for the new positions he has for us.

Joseph was sold into slavery, falsely accused, thrown into prison, and forsaken. But God used all of those events to prepare him to rule a kingdom. David was anointed to be king over Israel but then spent many years running for his life from Saul. He spent much of his time hiding in caves. But again, God was using that time to prepare him to be king. God will often use prisons and caves to bring us to a place of desperation where we learn to totally rely on him. Jesus also went through a wilderness experience to prepare Him for what God was asking Him to do.

When we know through experience that God loves us and is always working for our good, then we can trust Him even when we are going through difficult times. He does not forsake us in those times, but He is using those circumstances to prepare us for greater things. If we are unable to deal with our present difficulties, then how can He place even more responsibility on us, knowing that we will crack under the pressure of that new environment? God uses our circumstances to expose areas in our hearts where change is needed and to prepare us to handle greater responsibility.

Many people blame the devil when they are going through wilderness experiences. But remember, it was the Spirit who led Jesus into the wilderness. Once he was in the wilderness, God allowed the devil to tempt him. The devil's plan was to destroy Jesus, but God was actually using the devil to prepare Jesus to step into His destiny.

Before continuing, I want to acknowledge the existence of other sources of suffering that should not be included in our discussion of wilderness experiences. For example, we may bring suffering into our lives through our own poor choices. There are also times when others may bring suffering into our lives through their poor choices. Suffering may also come to us through sickness or accidents. As used here in this moment, wilderness experience refers to a season of testing ordained by God for our edification. Also realize that even when suffering comes to us through a source other than God, God is still with us during those times. He never forsakes us.

This may seem difficult to believe, **but wilderness experiences are a result of God's love for us.** Because he loves us, He will never ask us to do anything that He hasn't equipped us to do. And many times He uses wilderness experiences to bring forth that equipping.

Most of us usually moan and complain while going through these experiences, not realizing God's love for us or His plan for our lives. I hope that this chapter will shed some new light into your wilderness. Your Father doesn't want you to fail in your calling; He loves you and wants you to succeed in all you do. That's why He spends so much time and effort preparing you, so that you will not fail.

From the time that God first called me into full time ministry until I actually moved into it, twelve years had passed by. During that interim, I had no idea what God was up to. I actually thought that He had forgotten about me, or that maybe I had somehow missed Him.

But looking back now, I can see the love and the care that He put into preparing me for this position. All of the things that I went through in my personal life and even everything that I had to deal with on my job were all used by God to prepare me for full time ministry. Had He not done that, I know that I would have been destroyed by the pressure of dealing with all of the problems associated with leading this ministry.

Jesus could not have accomplished all that He did for us were He not secure in his Father's love. Neither will you be able to fulfill your destiny apart from His love. Jesus knew that the Father loved him. He only said and did what the Father showed Him because He trusted Him with his life. To the degree that you know the Father's love for you, you will trust Him with your life and say and do only what He shows you, no matter what that might be and no matter what the cost to you personally.

And when you know the Father's love for you, you will fall in love with Him. When you discover all that He has done and continues to do on your behalf, you won't be able to do anything else but love Him. After finding out who He really is and what He is really like, how could you not love Him? He is such an awesome God!

And you will also find yourself loving others the way that He does. You will be motivated and compelled by love. As the Apostle John said, **"We love because he first loved us."** And as Paul said in his second letter to the Corinthians, "For Christ's love compels us," and "From now on we regard no one from a worldly point of view."

9

The Father's Heart

One of the keys to understanding spiritual principles, even those found in the scriptures, is understanding the Father's heart. Many times people interpret the scriptures or their present circumstances incorrectly, simply because they do not have an understanding of the Father's heart. When you don't know or understand His heart, how can you properly interpret what He has said or what He is doing in your life? It is easier to figure out where a person is coming from when you personally know the person who is doing the speaking. Knowing the heart of a person can help you understand the point they are trying to make. Let's take a few moments to examine God's heart.

James 1:17—Every good and perfect gift is from above, coming down from the Father of the heavenly lights, who does not change like shifting shadows.

Imagine that! Every good and perfect gift comes from the Father. Our Father in heaven loves to give us good gifts. And everything He gives us is perfect. He has always been that way and always will be. He does not change. He is not a mean and stingy God as some suppose. He is a very generous and loving God.

Luke 11:11-13—"Which of you fathers, if your son asks for a fish, will give him a snake instead? Or if he asks for an egg, will give him

a scorpion? If you then, though you are evil, know how to give good gifts to your children, how much more will your Father in heaven give the Holy Spirit to those who ask him!"

Matthews's account of this same teaching says, **"... how much more will your Father in heaven give good gifts to those who ask him!"** Again, these scriptures clearly portray the Father as a very loving and giving God who desires to give good things to His children. We love to give good things to our children, and our love for them is imperfect. But the Father's love for us is perfect, and He is able to give us so much more than we can possibly give our children. He is not bound by the limitations that we are. He created, owns, and controls all things. The Father's heart is one that loves to give to His children.

Now let's look at another very important aspect of the Father's heart, specifically dealing with our eternal destination. There are those who, not knowing the Father's heart, believe God to be an angry God who is just waiting to punish people and throw them into hell. They believe that if they don't live up to His perfect standard, they will be eternally punished. They believe that if they die with unconfessed sin in their lives, they will spend eternity apart from Him. They do not see God as a loving Father, but as a strict disciplinarian who demands perfection. But what does the scripture say?

2 Peter 3:9—The Lord is not slow in keeping his promise, as some understand slowness. He is patient with you, not wanting anyone to perish, but everyone to come to repentance.

1 Timothy 2:3-4—This is good, and pleases God our Savior, who wants all men to be saved and to come to a knowledge of the truth.

Ezekiel 33:11—"Say to them, 'As surely as I live, declares the Sovereign Lord, I take no pleasure in the death of the wicked, but rather that they turn from their ways and live. Turn! Turn from your evil ways! Why will you die, O house of Israel?'"

Micah 7:18—Who is a God like you, who pardons sin and forgives the transgression of the remnant of his inheritance? You do not stay angry forever but delight to show mercy.

It is clear to me from these verses that the Father's heart does not wish that anyone would die and have to spend eternity in hell apart from Him. As a matter of fact, hell was created for Satan and his angels, not for mankind. The Father is grieved when people die who haven't accepted Jesus into their lives. And I believe He does everything He can possibly do to keep people from going to hell, short of forcing them to receive Him. I believe He reveals the truth to all people and gives them every opportunity to be saved, but sadly many still reject Him and **by their own choosing,** they spend eternity in a place of torment.

Those, too, who believe that they are constantly falling out of salvation do not understand the Father's heart. If our salvation is based upon our obedience, then none of us have any chance of getting into heaven, for all have sinned and fall short of the glory of God. Scripture says that **if we claim to be without sin, we deceive ourselves and the truth is not in us.** If salvation is based on our effort, then Jesus died on the cross for nothing.

The Father loved us so much that He sent His Son to pay the penalty for our sins, so that by believing in Him we could have eternal life.

That's his heart! It's not a heart that's looking for every little reason to throw us into hell. It's a heart that is looking for every reason to keep us from hell.

John 3:16-17—"For God so loved the world that he gave his one and only Son, that whoever believes in him shall not perish but have eternal life. For God did not send his Son into the world to condemn the world, but to save the world through him."

Understand that when this scripture refers to God sending his Son, it is referring to the Father. The Father so loved the world that He gave his Son, that we might have eternal life. The Father's heart was to sacrifice the best that He had to offer in order to provide for our salvation. He gave to us what was most valuable to Him, his only Son. And Jesus didn't come to condemn the world; He came to save it, through faith in Him.

God so desired to spend eternity with mankind that He himself came down to die in our place so that we could be reconciled to Him! What more could he possibly do? Consider the words of Paul in his letter to the Romans.

Romans 8:32—He who did not spare his own Son, but gave him up for us all—how will he not also, along with him, graciously give us all things?

If the Father loved us so much that He was not even willing to spare his own Son, don't you think that it's His desire to do everything He can to save us? If He is willing to sacrifice his only Son for our sakes, is there anything He won't do to rescue us from the pit of hell? Our salvation is not based on what we do, other than to believe; it is based upon what the Father did through the Son. And the reason He did it was to restore our relationship to Him that was lost through our sin. The Father's heart longs for intimate fellowship with his highest creation, mankind. And He was willing to pay the ultimate price to get us back.

1 John 5:11-13—And this is the testimony: God has given us eternal life, and this life is in his Son. He who has the Son has life; he who does not have the Son of God does not have life. I write these things to you who believe in the name of the Son of God so that you may know that you have eternal life.

True salvation is not just mere intellectual assent to the existence of Jesus. Even the demons believe in Jesus-and shudder! When we say that we believe in Jesus, we are saying that we believe in our hearts who He says He is and that we will do our best to follow Him. It is getting to know God personally, not just believing that He exists.

John 17:3—"Now this is eternal life: that they may know you, the only true God, and Jesus Christ, whom you have sent."

We must come to the cross in true repentance, and change our way of thinking. True repentance involves not only a turning away from our sin but also a change in the way we view things. It involves coming into agreement with what God says. Though salvation is a free gift from the Father, it is neither cheap nor easy. It comes with the cost of laying down one's life at the cross in order to follow Him.

If we really believe, then we will be willing to do it His way. And when we do that, He transforms us into a new creation and restores us into a right relationship with Him. Sadly, there are many in the church today who claim to be believers but who have never surrendered to the one they claim to believe in. They have a form of godliness but deny the power of the cross.

What about you today? Have you truly surrendered your life to Jesus Christ, or do you just have some form of religion? Has God truly made you a new creation, and does the fruit of your life bear witness to that fact? Scripture says that if anyone is in Christ, he is a new creation. Does that describe you? Are you living in a relationship with God, whereby you hear His voice and do your best to obey Him, counting on His grace when you fail? If not, then I want you to consider the words of Paul in his letter to the Ephesians.

Ephesians 1:13-14—And you also were included in Christ when you heard the word of truth, the gospel of your salvation. Having believed, you were marked in him with a seal, the promised Holy Spirit, who is a deposit guaranteeing our inheritance until the redemption of those who are God's possession-to the praise of his glory.

As the Apostle Paul declared, whenever we hear the word of truth, the gospel of Jesus, and believe it, we are saved. And the moment we are saved, God deposits His Spirit within us and makes us a new creation. And His Spirit within us is the guarantee of our inheritance.

If you have never truly done that, then I encourage you to ask Jesus to come into your heart right now and forgive you of your sins. Ask Him to fill you with His Spirit and empower you to walk in obedience to Him and to be a witness to others. Allow Him to transform you into who he wants you to be. Remember, God does not want anyone to perish!

I want to look at one final aspect of the Father's heart, though there are many more we could look at. It is His desire for us to be conformed to the image of His Son.

Romans 8:29—For those God foreknew he also predestined to be conformed to the likeness of his Son, that he might be the firstborn among many brothers.

God's heart is for every believer to be conformed to the image or likeness of Jesus. When people look at us and the fruit of our lives, God wants them to see Jesus. He wants us to love like Jesus, act like Jesus, and do the things that Jesus did.

Everywhere Jesus went on this earth, crowds followed Him. They were attracted to Him, because He loved them, and He had the power to save, heal, and deliver them. God wants us to be so much like Jesus that people will be drawn to us also. And He will use any and every means in order to mold us into the image of Christ. Just as Jesus learned obedience from the things He suffered, so are we to learn from the trials in our lives.

Hebrews 5:7-10—During the days of Jesus' life on earth, he offered up prayers and petitions with loud cries and tears to the one who could save him from death, and he was heard because of his reverent submission. Although he was a son, he learned obedience from what he suffered and, once made perfect, he became the source of

eternal salvation for all who obey him and was designated by God to be high priest in the order of Melchizedek.

God allowed Jesus to suffer many things while here on this earth in order to teach Him obedience. Jesus would cry out to God during those times and God would hear Him because Jesus submitted Himself to the Father's authority. Once His obedience was complete, even to the point of death on the cross, He became the source of salvation for all who obey Him.

God desires to do the same in our lives. He allows us to go through various trials and struggles in our lives in order to teach us obedience. As previously stated, God will not pour his glory into vessels that aren't prepared to carry it. He will not pour new wine into old wineskins, because He knows the wineskins will burst, and the wine will be lost. He wants us to move in the same love, compassion, and power that Jesus did. But in order for that to happen, He must first prepare us to do so. And He uses the trials, persecutions, and circumstances of our lives to refine us into people worthy of his glory.

And many times He allows our adversary, the devil, to bring these negative things into our lives. The devil's purpose is always to steal, kill, and destroy. But God wants to use these same issues to build character in us. The higher the quality of our character, the more glory He can pour through us. So God tests our faith in order to produce character.

James 1:2-3—Consider it pure joy, my brothers, whenever you face trials of many kinds, because you know that the testing of your faith develops perseverance. Perseverance must finish its work so that you may be mature and complete, not lacking anything.

Romans 5:3-5—Not only so, but we also rejoice in our sufferings, because we know that suffering produces perseverance; perseverance, character; and character, hope. And hope does not disappoint us, because God has poured out his love into our hearts by the Holy Spirit, whom he has given us.

God tests our faith because He loves us, and He wants to produce the same character in us that Jesus had. He knows that with great power and glory also come great pressure and responsibility. If He were to pour his glory into vessels that easily crack under pressure, then they would be destroyed. So He allows us to be tested in many ways in order to bring us to a place of maturity in our faith. He wants to see if we will abandon our faith in times of great trial, or if we will turn to Him and allow Him to give us even more faith through our perseverance.

The heart of God is searching for vessels to carry his glory here on the Earth. He so desires to pour out His love, power, and glory upon the Earth. But He chooses to do that through earthen vessels. So He puts them through "stress tests" to see if they will crack under the weight of His glory. He does it because He loves us, not because He is angry with us or punishing us. And when we understand this principle, we position ourselves to be the ones through whom He can pour out his glory on the Earth.

I have suffered many things since becoming a Christian. I nearly lost my leg to an infection, and I've dealt with the pain of kidney stones three times now, one of which required surgery to be removed. I have faced financial ruin and marriage problems which almost led to divorce. I have suffered with gout and severe heartburn. I had a very severe case of hemorrhoids, which also required surgery, and was the cause of extreme pain in my body for many days.

I have nearly lost my life on many occasions, and only by the grace of God am I here today. A foster child, whom we were trying to show love to, nearly shot my wife, Tina, and then stole our vehicle, and ran off with another foster child who lived next door. I lost my dad to heart disease, even though I believed that God was going to heal him. I have watched my wife and children, and others that I love dearly, suffer many things also, which hurts me more than my own pain. My wife and I also had to deal with the pain of having two miscarriages.

These are just a few of the trials that I have suffered, and all of them tested my faith and caused me to cry out to God and ask Him to move on my behalf. Many times I didn't understand at the time what was going on or why I was going through such difficult trials, but looking back now, I see that God was trying to produce perseverance and character in me. And He wants to do the same in you.

Please understand that these sicknesses and diseases were not put on me by God in order to produce character in me. They are the result of living in a fallen world. They are the result of the effects of sin upon the Earth for thousands of years. They are part of the war that we are in every day against the spiritual forces of evil in the heavenly realms. But God still used them to form me into the image of His Son.

I want to share with you a vision that I experienced just recently after our second miscarriage. The baby was due to be born in August of 2008, but we found out we lost him just after the New Year began. Our hearts were grieved, but I can honestly say that I never questioned why God would allow that to happen to us.

It was the Sunday immediately following the loss of our child. I went to church saddened in my heart and spirit but determined to worship the Lord despite my present circumstances. I wasn't into loud, excited, clapping and dancing type worship. I just wanted to be alone with my Father and spend some time in His presence. After only a few minutes into worship, I entered into this vision.

I saw the Father in heaven reach down and pick up a newborn baby. He held it up toward me and said, "This is your son, Benjamin." Benjamin Joseph was the name that I felt God had given us for our new baby. I began to cry as I watched the Father hold my son close to his chest.

Then I saw Benjamin sitting on the Father's lap, but now he was about three or four years old. He was a cute little guy with reddish blond hair. He asked God if his earthly father would have been a good Daddy. The Father replied, "One of the best." Then Benjamin asked Him what I was like. The Father said that I was a very loving and compassionate man who loved God very much. He said that He was using me to touch the lives of many lost and broken people here on the earth. Benjamin had a huge smile on his face as he listened to the Father. I was still in tears.

Next I saw Benjamin around the age of twelve. He was in training with a warrior angel. He was learning how to wield a sword, shoot a bow and arrows, throw a spear, and defend himself with a shield. The Father told me that he was training Benjamin to be a mighty warrior in the spiritual realm, just like his father.

The last time I saw Benjamin in this vision he was around eighteen years old. He had curly hair and looked very impressive. He was dressed in full battle armor, looking somewhat like a Roman soldier. He had the same fierce look in his eyes that I have seen in the eyes of Jesus in times past. The Lord spoke to me and said that everywhere I go to minister here on the Earth, he would send Benjamin there to do warfare on my behalf in the spiritual realm. How awesome is that!

Then the scene changed and I was watching a little black haired girl worshipping with some angels. She had such a beautiful voice. I asked the Lord who she was. He said she was my daughter, Samantha. She was the baby we lost in our first miscarriage. He said she would now be ten if she had stayed on the Earth. I continued to cry. Could it be that God has a special purpose for all of the unborn babies from the Earth?

I realize that I am sharing some incredible encounters with you in this book. It may be difficult to believe or understand some of these things. But I do not believe that any of my experiences go against the teachings of the scriptures. And I want you to realize that our quest to know God and understand His ways can be full of mystery.

But the promise of scripture is that those who seek Him with all of their hearts will find Him. And sometimes God uses these "mysteries" to separate those who truly want to know God from those who are just seeking knowledge. It is my sincere hope that in sharing my experiences, you will be drawn closer to Him and perhaps encounter Him yourself.

So what circumstances and situations are you dealing with in your life? Are you being wiped out by them, or do you see them as the "refiner's fire?" Are you seeking God for revelation and understanding, so that you can grow in your faith and be placed in new positions? Or are you blaming God for all of the terrible things that He is doing to you? Your perspective of these trials will make the difference in whether you pass the test and move on to bigger and better things, or whether you keep going around the same mountain being tested over and over again.

10

The Prodigal

Luke, Chapter 15, gives three separate accounts of things that were lost and then found again. In each account, there is great rejoicing when the lost items are found. And I believe all three of these accounts help reveal the Father's heart when it comes to dealing with mankind. For the sake of this chapter, we are going to briefly examine the third of the three accounts which is commonly known as the "Parable of the Lost Son."

Our purpose is not so much to examine every detail of this account as it is to simply explore the heart of the Father evidenced here.

Luke 15:11-32—Jesus continued: "There was a man who had two sons. The younger one said to his father, 'Father, give me my share of the estate.' So he divided his property between them.

Not long after that, the younger son got together all he had, set off for a distant country and there squandered his wealth in wild living. After he had spent everything, there was a severe famine in that whole country, and he began to be in need. So he went and hired himself out to a citizen of that country, who sent him to his fields to feed pigs. He longed to fill his stomach with the pods that the pigs were eating, but no one gave him anything.

When he came to his senses, he said, 'How many of my father's hired men have food to spare, and here I am starving to death! I

will set out and go back to my father and say to him: Father, I have sinned against heaven and against you. I am no longer worthy to be called your son; make me like one of your hired men.' So he got up and went to his father.

But while he was still a long way off, his father saw him and was filled with compassion for him; he ran to his son, threw his arms around him and kissed him.

The son said to him, 'Father, I have sinned against heaven and against you. I am no longer worthy to be called your son.'

But the Father said to his servants, 'Quick! Bring the best robe and put it on him. Put a ring on his finger and sandals on his feet. Bring the fattened calf and kill it. Let's have a feast and celebrate. For this son of mine was dead and is alive again; he was lost and is found.' So they began to celebrate.

Meanwhile, the older son was in the field. When he came near the house, he heard music and dancing. So he called one of the servants and asked him what was going on. 'Your brother has come,' he replied, 'and your father has killed the fattened calf because he has him back safe and sound.'

The older brother became angry and refused to go in. So his father went out and pleaded with him. But he answered his father, 'Look! All these years I've been slaving for you and never disobeyed your orders. Yet you never gave me even a young goat so I could celebrate with my friends. But when this son of yours who has

squandered your property with prostitutes comes home, you kill the fattened calf for him!'

'My son,' the father said, 'you are always with me, and everything I have is yours. But we had to celebrate and be glad, because this brother of yours was dead and is alive again; he was lost and is found.'"

Notice the response of the father in this account. First of all, he allowed the younger son to do as he pleased. He did not try to control him in any way. He allowed him to make his own decisions and to choose his own paths. Though I'm sure he was saddened by the decisions the son made, he gave him a free will to choose as he so desired.

Our Father in heaven also gives us a free will to make our own choices. And I'm sure He is grieved at some of the choices we make, yet He does not try to control us. He wants us to come to him by our own choosing, not because He forces us to. Nothing pleases him more than when a person chooses to love Him and follow Him.

And what was the father's response to the younger son after he had squandered all his wealth on wild living? Did he punish him for it? Did he criticize him for it? Did he kick him out of the house? Did he disown him? The answer to all of these questions is obviously, no! The father was watching and waiting for him to return, and while he was still a long way off, the father saw him coming and ran to him and kissed him. He had compassion on him. It didn't matter to the father what the son had done or where he had been, the only thing that mattered now was that the son had come home.

Many of us feel or believe that when we mess up, our Father is going to be mad at us. We think that He won't love us or accept us any longer. We fear that He is going to punish us. We feel we have gone too far and there is no longer any hope for us. But nothing could be further from the truth. He is waiting for us to return so He can have compassion on us. He wants to run to us and give us a big kiss also. He actually misses us and desires more for us to be with Him than he does to punish us. He doesn't hate us, and He doesn't throw us out of the family.

Not only that, but notice also how the father completely welcomed his prodigal son back into the family. He put the best robe on his son, just as our heavenly Father clothes us with the very best when He puts the righteousness of Christ on us. He put a ring on his finger, signifying that this son belonged to his family and had authority to act on behalf of the family. Then he threw a feast and celebrated his son's return. He was filled with joy to have his son back safe and sound!

That doesn't sound like an angry father who is waiting to punish his children every time they mess up. It sounds like our loving, heavenly Father, who is more concerned with having us in relationship with Him than punishing us for our sins.

I too was once a prodigal son. I had moved away from home and chosen to indulge myself in all the pleasures of this world. I considered it my duty to party and get drunk every night. I did drugs and I was addicted to pornography. I was living a lifestyle that was leading me directly to hell.

It seemed like I was having a great time on the outside, but inside I was dying. I was longing for love and tried everything that the world had to offer to find it. But there was none to be found in the world. I became so miserable in my inebriated lifestyle that many times I pondered how I might kill myself. I had no reason to live. I felt nobody loved me and my life wasn't worth a penny.

This was my condition when the love of the Father first found me. I didn't deserve His love, nor was I looking for it. But His love was searching for me. One night while I was driving back to my apartment, I was contemplating my life and thinking about killing myself. But then an unusual feeling came over me and I sensed something or someone was trying to get close to me.

So I cried out, **"God, if you are for real, then show me. If not, I can't go on."** I began to weep. I was so disgusted with my life. All of the sudden, I felt this presence come into my car. I couldn't see anybody, but I knew that God was sitting beside me in the front seat. I began to weep even more, so much so that I had to pull over on the side of the road.

Then the love of God began to engulf me, and for the first time in a long time it actually seemed like somebody cared about me. How could this be? So I asked, "God, how can you love me? Don't you know how sinful I am? Don't you realize what kind of person I am? Nobody could possibly love someone like me."

But God replied, "Rick, I love you so much that I sent my Son to die in your place so that you could have life." I wept and wept as the love of the Father just poured over me and into me. I could feel the burden of my sin and my wicked lifestyle lifting off of me.

Suddenly I was in a vision, and I found myself standing at the foot of the cross. I looked up at Jesus and He looked down at me. He said, "My love for you is so great that I am willing to endure the cross for your sake." As I looked into His eyes, I was overwhelmed by His love and once again my eyes filled with tears. **I could not understand how God could love me so much!** Even to this day it is hard for us to comprehend the love of God for us, but just because we can't understand it, doesn't change the fact that it is so.

I found myself back in my car again. I asked Jesus to come into my heart and forgive me of my sin, which He did. Words cannot describe the release of pain and burden that I experienced that night. But it was truly liberating. I had found the love that I had been searching for all of my life!

Hear me now. I don't care where you have been or what you have done. I don't care how messed up you think your life might be. I don't care how much sin you have committed. You have a Father in heaven who loves you more than you can imagine. You have a Savior named Jesus who loves you so much that He took the penalty for your sin so that you could be reconciled to the Father. You have the Holy Spirit who is trying to lead you back to God. Even if you were already a Christian but have fallen away, you have a loving Father who is waiting for you with open arms to welcome you back into the family.

I encourage you to take time **RIGHT NOW** and ask the Father to show you His love. If you have never asked Jesus to come into your heart and forgive you of your sins, then now is the time. If you have fallen away, then now is the time to come to your senses and return to the Father. He is watching and waiting for all of you. He wants to throw a feast on your behalf. He wants you to be his child, so he can pour his love and goodness upon you. What are you waiting for? Run to him now!

11

The Father's Will

Throughout Old Testament times, there was a certain viewpoint of God that permeated the beliefs of the people. God seemed very distant and unapproachable to them. They knew little about him, partly because God had not yet revealed His fullness to man. And many people were fearful of God.

Consider the Israelites at Mount Sinai when Moses went up to receive the Ten Commandments. They told Moses to go up on the mountain and listen to what God says, then come down and tell them what He said. They were afraid to get near to God themselves.

There were a few who new God intimately, like Abraham, Moses, and David, but most people really had no concept of who God was. Most viewed Him as a Judge, who was ready to pronounce judgment the moment any of his laws were broken. That is one of the reasons God sent His Son, to give us a full revelation of the Father.

Galatians 4:4-7—But when the time had fully come, God sent his Son, born of a woman, born under law, to redeem those under law, that we might receive the full rights as sons. Because you are sons, God sent the Spirit of his Son into our hearts, the Spirit who calls out, "*Abba*, Father." So you are no longer a slave, but a son; and since you are a son, God has made you also an heir.

The Father's will in sending his Son was to redeem us (buy us back) from under the law so that we could become His sons and daughters, having the full rights of an heir. It was His will to reveal Himself as a loving Father; hence the term *Abba* was used, indicating how the Father now wanted us to view Him. *Abba* was a term of endearment used by Jewish children to refer to their earthly dads. God no longer wanted us to see Him according to the previous views of who He was. Jesus came to give us the full revelation of the Father.

This is one of the most important truths in the entire universe, that we learn to see God as our loving Father. Without this divine revelation, there is no life, there is no love, and there is no hope for any of us. It is the Father who holds the universe in His hands and controls all things. It is this same Father who holds us in the palm of His hands. Bringing this revelation to us is one of the primary reasons Jesus came.

Matthew 11:27—"All things have been committed to me by my Father. No one knows the Son except the Father, and no one knows the Father except the Son and those to whom the Son chooses to reveal him."

In John chapter 8, the people asked Jesus who He was. He said He was who He was claiming to be all along. He said the one who sent Him was reliable, and that He would tell the world what He had heard from Him. But they did not understand that He was telling them about His Father. You see, before that time, no one had ever spoken of God as Father. But now Jesus was trying to reveal His Father to all mankind.

John 14:6-9—Jesus answered, "I am the way, the truth, and the life. No one comes to the Father except through me. If you really knew me, you would know my Father as well. From now on, you do know him and have seen him." Phillip said, "Lord, show us the Father and that will be enough for us." Jesus answered: "Don't you know me, Phillip, even after I have been among you such a long time? Anyone who has seen me has seen the Father."

In the book of Luke, Chapter 11, we have the account of the disciples asking Jesus to teach them how to pray. Notice who Jesus said they should address their prayers to. Again, he was trying to change the way they viewed the Father. He was trying to show them, and us, that their heavenly Father cared about them and would answer their prayers.

Luke 11:2—He said to them, "When you pray, say: Our Father in heaven, hallowed be your name."

Throughout His ministry here on the earth, Jesus kept emphasizing how we were now to view Father. We were to come to the Father, know the Father, pray to the Father, and love the Father. He said He would show us the way to the Father. He said the Father was the source of life for all people. Everything that Jesus did He did in obedience to the Father. So everything He did was the Father's will.

I want to explore another important aspect of the Father's will. We know that Jesus was sent by the Father to die on the cross, making it possible for all people to be forgiven of their sin and receive eternal life. This was certainly one of the primary purposes for which Jesus was sent, along with revealing the Father to people. But I want to focus on another very important part of the ministry of Jesus while He was here on the earth, in order to reveal the will of the Father.

John 6:38—"For I have come down from heaven not to do my will but to do the will of him who sent me."

Certainly the biggest part of God's plan in sending Jesus was for Him to die on our behalf so that we could be reconciled to the Father. But if we look at all that Jesus did in his earthly ministry before He gave his life, we can see another important part of doing the Father's will. Simply put, it was and still is the Father's will for all people to be saved, healed, and delivered from the power of the enemy.

Matthew 4:23-24—Jesus went throughout Galilee, teaching in their synagogues, preaching the good news of the kingdom, and healing every disease and sickness among the people. News about him spread all over Syria, and people brought to him all who were ill with various diseases, those suffering severe pain, the demon-possessed, those having seizures, and the paralyzed, and he healed them.

Everywhere Jesus went, He preached the good news of the kingdom, healed the sick, and drove out demons. This was all to fulfill his Father's will. It is God's will for all people to be made completely whole; for them to healed physically, spiritually, and emotionally. Jesus came to make us whole; in body, soul, and spirit. This was His Father's will. And it was what Isaiah had prophesied about Jesus hundreds of years earlier.

Isaiah 53:4-5—Surely he took up our infirmities and carried our sorrows, yet we considered him stricken by God, smitten by him, and afflicted. But he was pierced for our transgressions, he was crushed for our iniquities; the punishment that brought us peace was upon him, and by his wounds we are healed.

There are many who believe that these verses pertain to only our spiritual healing, in other words, for our salvation. But these verses also say that Jesus took up our infirmities (sicknesses, diseases) and carried our sorrows (fears, rejection, depression). He provided for the healing of our bodies and our souls as well. The proof of this understanding of these verses is found in the New Testament.

Matthew 8:16-17—When evening came, many who were demon possessed were brought to him, and he drove out the spirits with a word and healed all the sick. This was to fulfill what was spoken through the prophet Isaiah: "He took up our infirmities and carried our diseases."

Do you see it? It is the Father's will for all people to be saved, healed, and set free from demonic oppression. Not only did Jesus do these things while he ministered on the earth, but he also sent out his twelve disciples to do the same.

Matthew 10:1—He called his twelve disciples to him and gave them authority to drive out evil spirits and to heal every disease and sickness.

Matthew 10:7-8—"As you go, preach this message: 'The kingdom of heaven is near.' Heal the sick, raise the dead, cleanse those who

have leprosy, drive out demons. Freely you have received, freely give."

Imagine that! Jesus sent out his disciples and told them to preach the same message of the kingdom that He was preaching. And He told them to do the same things that He was doing, including healing the sick and driving out demons. He even went as far as to tell them to raise the dead. And later on He sent out not just the twelve, but seventy-two of his disciples and He gave them the same message and told them to do the same things again. Notice that Jesus gave them authority to heal every disease and sickness. This is hard for some of us to believe, but I believe it is God's will for all to be healed. And I pray and minister as such.

Now consider the last commandment that Jesus gave to his disciples before he ascended into Heaven. I believe these verses include us today because they still speak of the Father's will.

Mark 16:15-18—He said to them, "Go into all the world and preach the good news to all creation. Whoever believes and is baptized will be saved, but whoever does not believe will be condemned. And these signs will accompany those who believe: In my name they will drive out demons; they will speak in new tongues; they will pick up snakes with their hands; and when they drink deadly poison, it will not hurt them at all; they will place their hands on sick people, and they will get well."

12

What About Me?

I often get asked questions like, "How can I experience God like you do?" or "What do I need to do to have encounters like you?" Unfortunately, there is no simple answer to these questions. In today's society, people are always looking for a three, five, or ten step program that they can follow to achieve the same results as someone else did. But there are no such programs in the kingdom of God. The kingdom of God is not a matter of following programs; it is all about living in relationships with God and with other people.

In ministering to a variety of people over the years, I have found that there is a real tendency in people to want someone else to do all the work and then provide them with a simple formula they can follow to success. They don't want to invest valuable time into something when somebody else already has the solution. They often want someone to hear from God for them, which takes the responsibility off of themselves and puts it onto another person.

The following statement is a simple truth that I believe. If you want to experience God the way that I do, then you are going to have to log the time for yourself. You are going to have to spend time in worship, prayer, searching the scriptures, and communion with God. And you must do those things not out of a religious mindset, but out of a sincere desire to deepen your relationship with God.

That's what a relationship is. It is two way communication—sharing your heart with God and taking time to listen for Him to share what's on His heart with you. You can't have a relationship with God through someone else. Though others may help you at times with your relationship, they can't have a relationship for you. It's up to you.

Having said all of that, I want to offer some insights to you that I have learned over the years that may help you in your relationship with God. But please understand, this is not a program or formula that will guarantee your success. These are simply tips to help you grow in your relationship with the Father. And hopefully, you will encounter Him as I and many others do.

One of the keys that God showed me a number of years ago is humility. The Lord led me to the book of Numbers one day in order to teach me about humility.

Numbers 12:5-8—Then the Lord came down in a pillar of cloud; he stood at the entrance to the Tent and summoned Aaron and Miriam. When both of them stepped forward, he said, "Listen to my words: When a prophet of the Lord is among you, I reveal myself to him in visions, I speak to him in dreams. But this is not true of my servant Moses; he is faithful in all my house. With him I speak face to face, clearly and not in riddles; he sees the form of the Lord."

As I pondered these verses, I began to realize that I had a prophetic gift and that many times God had given me dreams and visions, just as the scripture said. But I wanted God to speak to me like He did to

Moses. Though I greatly appreciated every dream and vision, I wanted God to speak to me clearly.

Many times dreams and visions require interpretation, which allows for error through our own misunderstanding, our flesh, or even the influence of the enemy. I wanted God to speak to me face to face, as with Moses. So I asked the Lord why it was that He spoke face to face with Moses, clearly, and not in riddles. He told me to go back and read verse three.

Numbers 12:3—Now Moses was a very humble man, more humble than anyone else on the face of the earth.

The Lord spoke to me and said, **"Rick, if you will humble yourself like Moses did, then I will speak with you as I did with him."** His words penetrated deep into my soul and spirit. I knew this was a major revelation and that if I could somehow grasp what God was saying, then He would reveal Himself to me in ways I had never known.

This revelation has had a profound impact on my life. It was so important to me, that years later, when I started this ministry, I called it **"Humble Heart Life Ministries."** I wanted to keep the revelation of humility ever in front of my eyes. If you want to encounter God face to face, as I often do, then I believe one of the most important keys is humility.

Let me give you my understanding of humility. First of all, humility is not weakness. It is not letting everyone and everything walk all over you. There is actually great strength in humility. But that strength is not your own, it comes from the Lord.

Humility involves an acknowledgment of our sinfulness and our weakness, but it also involves acknowledging His forgiveness and His strength. It involves submission to God and obedience to Him. It involves acknowledging God in everything we do, and not relying on our own understanding. There are two scriptures that seem to sum up my belief about humility:

Apart from him, we can do nothing, and **I can do all things through Christ who strengthens me.**

I also believe that **Proverbs 3:5-6** offers a great way of defining humility.

Trust in the Lord with all your heart, and lean not on your own understanding. In all your ways acknowledge him, and he will direct your paths.

I truly believe that if we will acknowledge God in everything we do, He will reveal Himself to us and show us His ways. And what does it mean to acknowledge Him?

It means to ask Him what His desire or His will is in all that we do. It means not making any decisions or doing anything without first seeking Him and hearing from Him. Though I am not perfect, this is how I try to live my life. And remember, the Bible says that God opposes the proud but gives grace to the humble.

I also want you to understand that I do make some decisions without asking God. There are some decisions that we make on a daily basis that do not require His direction. For instance, I don't ask Him what clothes I should wear everyday or what I should eat for breakfast. These are questions that do not require His attention. But anything that relates to His will and direction for our lives, or when and how we should minister to someone, should be run through Him first.

There are three scriptures that sum up the next point I want to make. Since God gave me this revelation, I have relied heavily upon these scriptures to give me access into the heavenly realms. And I believe that if you grasp this revelation, it will open the way for you to enter that realm also.

Matthew 27:51—At that moment the curtain of the temple was torn in two from top to bottom.

The curtain of the temple was what separated the Holy Place from the Holy of Holies. The priests were allowed to enter the Holy Place, but only the high priest could enter the Holy of Holies, and he could only do that once a year after fulfilling the sacrifices and regulations that were required. The Holy of Holies is where the presence of God dwelt. And so up until that time, only the high priest had access to the very presence of God.

But when God tore the curtain in two from top to bottom, He was saying that now everyone could enter into His presence any time they wanted. Jesus had made it possible for ordinary people like you and me to access the Father through His death on the cross. The demands of the law had been met forever, and now through the blood of Jesus we have access to the very presence of Almighty God. Consider what the writer of Hebrews had to say about this.

Hebrews 10:19-22—Therefore, brothers, since we have confidence to enter the Most Holy Place by the blood of Jesus, by a new and living way opened for us through the curtain, that is, his body, and since we have a great priest over the house of God, let us draw near to God with a sincere heart in full assurance of faith, having our hearts sprinkled to cleanse us from a guilty conscience and having our bodies washed with pure water.

We can boldly and confidently enter into the presence of God, not because of righteous things that we have done, not because we earned it or deserve it, but simply because of the blood of Jesus. His blood alone is what makes us worthy to enter into the Father's presence. I have so many people tell me they don't feel worthy to enter His presence, or that they feel guilty because of their sin. But the blood of Jesus has cleansed us from a guilty conscience and has washed us with pure water, making us clean.

Now let's look at the third scripture that I mentioned earlier.

Revelation 4:1—After this I looked, and there before me was a door standing open in heaven. And the voice I had first heard speaking to me like a trumpet said, "Come up here, and I will show you what must take place after this."

It is my belief that every revelation and encounter that I find in scripture is available to me. God is not a respecter of persons, and His word is relevant for all people. What truth is available to one is available to all. So when God gave me this revelation, I believed it was available to me.

The door to heaven is standing open, and Jesus is calling to us to "come up here." I said to the Lord that if the door was open for John, then it must also be open for me. He told me that I was correct. So I began to ask Him to take me into the heavenly realms and I believed that He would. And wouldn't you know it! I began to have heavenly encounters that continue to this day. God willing, I will share the details of some of these encounters in future books.

There is one final key that I want to explore in this chapter. We have already looked at the importance of humility and accessing the Father through the blood of Jesus. Now I want to focus on a third aspect, which involves getting the Father to look in our direction and hear our cries. Please understand that we cannot control or manipulate God into doing what we want, but I do believe that we can sway Him in our direction. And I believe the key to doing that is our passion for Him.

2 Chronicles 16:9—For the eyes of the Lord range throughout the earth to strengthen those whose hearts are fully committed to him.

God is looking for people whose hearts are fully committed to Him. He is looking for those who are passionate towards Him. Though he loves all people the same, His eyes are always searching for those who love Him more than anyone or anything else. These are the ones that He desires to reveal Himself to. These are the ones who get His attention.

The Bible says that our Maker is our Husband. As a husband, I desire my wife to be passionate towards me. And I can honestly say that the more passionate she is towards me, the more I desire to be with her and to do things for her. It's not that my love for her ever changes, but my passion for her and my desire to please her does. Her passion is the key to accessing my heart.

I believe it is the same with God. Our passion for Him can be an important key to accessing his heart. The entire book of the Song of Solomon describes the type of passionate love that exists between a husband (God) and a bride (us) who truly love each other. This is the way God wants our relationship to be with Him. And I believe our passion for Him will incline his heart toward us and will cause Him to desire to reveal Himself to us.

When we are truly and passionately in love with someone, our desire is to do things for them that are pleasing to them. We lay down our own selfish ambitions in order to fulfill their needs and desires. Life is no longer all about us, but it's about pleasing the one we deeply love. We no longer desire what we can get from them; we desire what we can give to them. And when we love them in that manner, then they tend to return their love to us in the same way. When we passionately love God, He can't help but desire to reveal Himself to us in ways that others don't experience. Seek His face, not His hands.

As a Father, nothing gets my attention quicker than when one of my children is hurt and crying out for help. I will do everything in my power to help them in any way that I can. And I believe it is the same way for our Father in heaven towards us. When we cry out for help, He comes running. When the enemy is picking on us, Daddy comes to the rescue, if we allow Him to. Stop trying to handle everything yourself and cry out to Daddy for help.

I also cannot stress enough the importance of having intimate time alone with Him. Did you notice the word alone in the last sentence? Our daily lives are filled with so many things that take up all of our time so that we have no time for God. And when we do go to Him in prayer, we tend to give Him a laundry list of everything we want Him to do for us and then we move on to something else. We never take the time to listen for Him to speak to us.

Much of my "prayer time" these days is spent just listening for Him to speak to me. Some people call it "soaking." I don't care what you call it, but I encourage you to do it. He already knows all of our needs so I have learned to just seek Him and ask Him what's on His heart. Is there anything you want to show me God? How can I please you today?

Many times I start by asking God to forgive me of my sins and to remove from me any walls that would separate me from Him. I often put on some worship music and just lie down in His presence listening for His voice. I tell Him that I want more of Him in my life, and less of me. I ask Him to take me to where He is. And many times He does!

So again, this is not a three step formula to induce heavenly encounters. But I believe that if you do these things from your heart, and not from a religious mindset, that you can incline God's ear toward you. Humble yourself before the Lord. Believe that you have access to the heavenly realms through the blood of Jesus and ask Him to take you there. Be passionate toward God and cry out to Him as a child to his father. And maybe you will suddenly find yourself in His presence. There is no greater place to be!

13

Fatherhood

If ever there was a time on the earth when there was a need for a revelation of the Father's love, it is now. Our world is so full of hatred, and I'm not just talking about in the unbelieving world. Even in the "church" today there are many people full of bitterness, resentment, and unforgiveness. The words of Jesus about what it will be like in the last days certainly ring true in our society.

Matthew 24:10-12—"At that time many will turn away from the faith and will betray and hate each other, and many false prophets will appear and deceive many people. Because of the increase of wickedness, the love of most will grow cold."

There is such a lack of love in our world today. And there are so many people who suffer from love deficits in their lives. There are so many broken marriages and broken homes, which means broken moms, broken dads, and broken children. I find myself constantly ministering to divorced women and single moms. The enemy has launched an all out attack on families in an attempt to destroy the most fundamental and basic unit of relationship that God has established, the family. I praise God for women who are trying to fulfill the role of both parents with their children.

God has given me so much love and compassion for both men and women who are dealing with this issue. We know that many women suffer deep emotional wounds when their marriages fall apart, but I know that many men do too. They put on this "tough guy" image and act like everything is ok, but deep down inside they are hurting also. Typically, the reason why both individuals are acting the way they are and doing what they are doing to each other is because they both have wounds inside that have never been dealt with. It is important that we try to minister to the needs of everyone involved in these situations.

God established families in order to provide the love, security, affirmation, and purpose that every individual needs. And that's not only true in the physical sense, but also in the spiritual sense. The entire kingdom of God is all about our becoming a part of God's family, living in a loving relationship with Him and with our brothers and sisters in Christ. And I believe that the key person in every family is the father.

The father is the one who is supposed to provide the love, security (protection and provision), affirmation (value), and purpose that the other members of the family need. And when the father isn't fulfilling his calling in any of these areas, then the whole family suffers. It is no wonder why the enemy has done everything in his power to destroy the family unit by removing the fathers from the family. There are so many wives struggling through life without their husbands and so many children growing up these days without the presence of a father figure in their lives.

The Lord recently spoke to me and said, **"I need you to be a father to a fatherless generation."** There are so many people who have never experienced the love of a father because they grew up without one.

They neither understand nor submit to authority, because the authority figure of their lives wasn't there. They live in fear, not knowing what it is like to have a father's protection and provision. And they have no self esteem, because they didn't receive any affirmation from their father. This is true not only in our physical families but also in our spiritual family. As previously discussed in chapter six, there are many in the church today who don't know or understand our heavenly Father, because of the type of relationship that they had with their earthly father.

I believe we are living in a day when God is restoring the office of apostles. We have already seen the restoration of the prophets, and now God is bringing back the final office of the fivefold ministry. And I truly believe that one of the most important rules of the apostles in these last days will be to father this generation. Too many people have grown up as orphans, not having any spiritual father. Consider the words of Paul to the Corinthian church.

1 Corinthians 4:15—Even though you have ten thousand guardians in Christ, you do not have many fathers, for in Christ Jesus I became your father through the gospel.

Even in Paul's day, there was a great need for spiritual fathers. There were many guardians, but few fathers. As an apostle, Paul knew the importance of people having father figures in their lives. And in today's society, many generations removed from that one, the need is even greater. It is imperative that those who are called to be apostles today truly model what it means to be a spiritual father. And I believe that is what God is trying to restore to the church in our day.

Malachi 4:5-6—"See, I will send you the prophet Elijah before that great and dreadful day of the Lord comes. He will turn the hearts of the fathers to their children, and the hearts of the children to their fathers."

My goal in raising my four children is to show them what a father's love is truly all about. I am trying to raise them the way that my heavenly Father raises me. I want them to know the value of submitting to me as the authority figure in their lives. And in return for their submission, I provide the love, security, affirmation, and purpose that they need. This is the way my heavenly Father is with me. He provides for all of my needs, and all He asks in return is that I submit to His authority.

In order for us to receive all of the benefits that our heavenly Father offers us, we must be willing to submit ourselves to Him as sons and daughters. The first part of that is to receive Him as our Lord and Savior, which brings us into the family of God and makes us sons and daughters of the King. But though we become children of God, we won't fully receive all of the benefits that He is offering us unless we are willing to submit to His parental authority.

On December 27th, 2007, at 2:30 am, the Father appeared to me in my bedroom. I have been visited by Jesus, the Holy Spirit, and angels many times in the past, but this was the first time that the Father showed up in my bedroom. He spoke to me for about two hours, and after He left, I crawled out of bed and recorded His words. He gave me a prophetic word and a vision for a woman who was struggling with the issue of the Father's love in her life. The day before that she had emailed me and shared her heart with me. I emailed her back and told her that I would not answer her question until I heard from God, though a number of thoughts of how to answer her went through my mind.

I knew the truth that she needed to hear, but I also knew that she had heard it before and it wouldn't mean much to her. She needed to hear directly from the Father on this one. I knew a word directly from Him would penetrate her heart and mind and set her free. Imagine how much God loves people that he actually appeared to me and gave me a direct word for her! I shared it with her a few days later and I believe it had a tremendous impact on her life. She was in tears as the Father ministered to her heart and spoke of issues that only He would know about. That's the type of Father he is!

He also spoke to me about what he desired for me to do. Here is a part of what the Father told me.

"You must share my love with everyone that I put in front of you. I am going to open doors for you to give you an opportunity to give to others what I am freely giving to you. Take the message of my love to those who are without it. My love will penetrate even the coldest hearts and will break down even the strongest walls around people's hearts. My love never fails.

Introduce me to people who think that they have met me but really haven't. For there are many who claim to know me but they really have no clue what I am all about. All they have is religion, and I am grieved that so many are missing out on a wonderful relationship with me.

I sent my Son to reconcile the world to Me. My Son came to reveal Me to the world. But the enemy has deceived people just as he did Adam and Eve. He wants people to be religious, and to fill their lives with religious activities, as long as they don't really become who I have called them to be. What he fears the most is people who truly learn to become my children and submit to me as their Father. Those who find their identity in me are the ones who do the most damage to Satan's kingdom.

Even creation itself is crying out for the sons of God to be revealed. But in order to be a son, you must first have a revelation of the Father. You must experience the love and security that is found only in your Daddy's arms. This is what Fatherhood is all about.

So go now, My son, and share the love that I have given to you with others. Show them who I really am and tell them of My great love for them. Love them, even as I have loved you."

My hearts desire is to do just that. Lord, help me to fulfill this commission that you have given me. Help me to reveal you to a world that desperately needs you but doesn't even know it yet.

My goal in ministry is to reveal the Father to and be a father to the people that God puts in front of me. I want to show them the importance of living in relationship. I want them to know the Father's love, his provision, and all his blessings. I want to teach them the importance of submitting to God. I want them to feel secure in my care and in His loving arms. I want them to know that they can come to me or to Him at any time for any reason to find help, or comfort, or whatever their need might be. I want them to know that they won't be judged or criticized, but that they will always be loved. I want them to experience "Fatherhood."

14

Sonship

We have nearly reached the end of our journey through this book. I have tried to reveal to you what I have received from the Lord concerning His love, His character, His heart, and His will. I have shared both personal encounters and revelation from the Father Himself. What you have received will have a great impact on your life, if you believe it and put it into practice.

It is time to set aside all of your preconceived notions about God and allow Him to reveal Himself to you. Forget what you have heard about Him in the past, and ask Him to give you a new revelation of Himself. Ask Him to remove all of the lies about Him from your mind and to renew your mind with the truth. Ask Him to give you a new revelation about his love. Begin to look to Him as the Father you always wanted and needed. In order to do that, you must be willing to humble yourself and submit to Him as a son or daughter. You must be willing to admit your weakness and your need for parental love and authority.

Most people have a hard time doing that because of their distorted views of their parents and other authority figures in their lives. Because of that distortion, they view God as distant and unapproachable. Some see Him as very strict, demanding, and hard to please. They feel they will never be good enough to get His approval. They feel unworthy to receive His love, and they fear being punished. But as we have seen, nothing could be further from the truth.

One of the things that we have to remember is that God knew everything about us before He chose us. It's not like He chose us and then later realized that He had made a horrible mistake. He knew our past, our present, and our future. He knew our sin, our weaknesses, and our failures. He knew how many times we would fall short and disappoint Him. But despite this foreknowledge, He still loves us and chooses to accept us just the way we are.

Our worth to Him is not determined by anything we have done in the past or by anything we will ever do in the future. He can't love us any more or any less than He already does. Nothing we do, either good or bad, can change His unfailing love for us, because His love is perfect and His love is unconditional. Our value to Him is solely based on what Jesus did for us on the cross. There is nothing we can do to add to that value. The only proper thing to do is to receive His love and enter into sonship.

John 1:12-13—Yet to all who received him, to those who believed in his name, he gave the right to become children of God—children born not of natural descent, nor of human decision or a husband's will, but born of God.

Try to imagine what it is like to be a son or daughter of the Creator of the universe, the Lord God Almighty! Imagine living life as a prince or princess; that is what we are. We are children of the King of Kings and Lord of Lords! We are royalty. We are the head and not the tail. We are blessed and not cursed. We are loved and not rejected. We have not only been saved from our sin, but we have been adopted by the God and Father of our Lord Jesus Christ. And we now have received the full rights of sons. Let us choose to live accordingly.

I encourage you to quit trying to earn what you already have been freely given, the gift of sonship. The more you try to earn it, the less you will have of it. Quit trying to prove your worth. God already established it when he sent Jesus to die on the cross. There is nothing you can do to add to it, and any attempt to do so is only self-righteousness. It is choosing to live under the law of sin and death instead of under grace.

Romans 8:19—The creation waits in eager expectation for the sons of God to be revealed.

All of creation itself is waiting for us to mature into the true sons and daughters of God. Though we became sons and daughters when we accepted Jesus into our hearts, creation is waiting for us to grow up. God doesn't want us to live as babies all of our lives, where we constantly need someone else to feed us and change our diapers. He wants us to become mature so He can give us the keys of the kingdom. He wants to know that He can trust us with them.

All of my children are heirs of everything that I have and own. But I am not going to give my eight year old son the keys to my truck and let him drive it. I am not going to hand him my checkbook and tell him to pay the bills. He is too small and too immature for that right now. But someday when he is old enough and mature enough, I will give him the keys. So it is with God. He is not going to give keys to people who are too immature to handle them.

Scripture speaks of a progression from slaves, to friends, to sons. Slaves typically have to beg their masters to get what they want. Friends ask if it is ok to do something. But sons give commands and they happen. Mature sons have been given the full authority of the father to act on behalf of the family business because the father knows he can trust them.

Many Christians live their entire lives as slaves, always begging God to do something for them. Some live as friends, asking God to move on their behalf. This is better, but not best. Sons know the heart, character, and will of their Father, and they speak and command into existence the things of the kingdom. They have the mind of Christ, and Father God trusts them to use their authority to work on behalf of the kingdom.

So which one are you most of the time? What do you need to do to truly become mature sons and daughters of God? Here are some helpful tips:

Learn to live in His love. It will help you to overcome all of the fear in your life. Trust Him with all of your heart, even when you are going through difficult times. He is working for your good. Allow Him to use the circumstances in your life to conform you to the image of his Son.

Believe the word of God. Believe both in what the scriptures say and also what he speaks to you personally. Quit listening to the lies of the enemy and start believing the truth of God. The truth will set you free.

Humble yourself before the Lord. Do not be afraid to expose yourself to Him, but allow Him set you free of the things that you are ashamed of in your life. Find someone who will love you and accept you the way you are, so that you can pray for each other and receive healing.

Believe that you also can access the heavenly realms. God does not show favoritism. He loves us all the same. You are worthy to enter His presence through the blood of Jesus. Go for it! Just be careful not to seek the experience more than the giver of the experience.

Be passionate for God. Seek Him with all of your heart. Spend time with Him. Love Him. Express your love to Him. Allow Him to fill you with His love.

I want to close this writing by sharing some truths from scripture with you. I have paraphrased them and changed the order of which they appear in the Bible in order to group ideas together. I pray that you will take them to heart and combine them with faith so that you will gain an understanding of how much God really loves you.

Your Father in heaven loves you more than you will ever be able to understand. He is for you, not against you. He desires for you to know Him personally, and intimately. He longs for fellowship with you, just as any earthly father who really loves his children desires to spend time with them. He wants to provide for your every need; physically, emotionally, and spiritually. He will comfort t you in all your trials.

He wants to share the secrets of his kingdom with you. He wants to pour out His power and glory through you. He wants to use you to be a blessing to others. He has a great plan for your life, to prosper you and not to harm you. He wants you to become mature so he can give you the keys of the kingdom.

You are His treasured possession. You are the apple of His eye, and the pearl of great price. There is nothing in all of creation that can separate you from His love. He loves you with an everlasting love. He loves you even as He loved His own son, Jesus.

He knows everything about you; even the hairs on your head are numbered. You were created in His image. You were fearfully and wonderfully made. It was God who determined the exact times and places you would live, so that you might reach out to Him and find Him.

His thoughts toward you are as countless as the sands on the seashore. You are His bride, beautifully adorned and prepared for His coming.

You are holy and blameless in His sight, without blemish, and free from accusation. He is not counting your sins against you, and He remembers them no more.

He is the Father that you have been searching for your entire life. You have tried everything that the world has to offer to fill the void in your heart, but nothing has worked. Now it is time for you to turn to Him. He is waiting and watching for you. He wants to throw a celebration on your behalf. If you seek him with all of your heart, you will find him.

My prayer for you is that you will truly experience **"The Father's Love."**

To contact us:
Rick Sodmont
834 Number Nine Road
Hastings, PA 16646
(814)247-8645 or
(814)243-7580

Email: ricksodmont@hotmail.com

Website: humbleheartlifeministries.com

978-0-595-50144-1
0-595-50144-3

CPSIA information can be obtained
at www.ICGtesting.com
Printed in the USA
LVHW010914190222
711538LV00005B/199